A Collection of Articles by
CAL GOLUMBIC

Just A Country Boy

Copyright © 1989-2024 by E. Calvin Golumbic
First Edition
First Printing

Volume 1 Hardcover ISBN: 979-8-218-50621-6

Printed in United States of America

No part of this publication may be reproduced, stored in a retrieval system, or transmitted in any form or by any means, electronic, mechanical, photocopying, recording, scanning, or otherwise, without the prior written permission of the author. This publication is designed to provide accurate and authoritative information in regards to the subject matter covered. It is sold with the understanding that neither the author nor the publisher is engaged in rendering legal, investment, accounting, or other professional services. While the author has used their best efforts in preparing this book, they make no representations or warranties with respect to the accuracy or completeness of the contents of this book and specifically disclaim any implied warranties of merchantability or fitness for a particular purpose. No warranty may be created or extended by sales representatives or written sales materials. The advice and strategies contained herein may not be suitable for your situation. You should consult with a professional when appropriate. The author shall be liable for any loss of profit or any other commercial damages, including but not limited to special, incidental, consequential, personal, or other damages.

Publishing Assistance provided by:
Heimat Publishing, Crystal Heidel

Dedicated to Clinton County and the County
Seat of Lock Haven, Pennsylvania.

Table of Contents

The First Day of Trout Season 3
Real Men Don't See Doctors 9
Lessons Learned 15
A Halloween Horror 19
Saturday Night 23
The Girl Next Door 29
Raising Your Parents 35
Pontiac Madness 41
The Lemont Band Hall 47
My Best Friend 53
The Wirehaired Terror 57
Capture the Flag 63
My Education 69
The Christmas Gift 75
Almost Heaven 81
Teen Angel 85
Learning to Drive 91
My 40th High School Reunion 97
Thanksgiving, Bah, Humbug! 101
The Godfather 107
Being Different 113
Recess 119
Peter's Steps 125
The Guy in the Mirror 131
A Town, a Trout, and a Tall Tale 137
Growing Up 143
Learning to Ride a Bicycle 149
Just Like Old Times 155
The Wind Beneath My Wings 161

The First Day of Trout Season
April, Year Unknown

The First Day of Trout Season

Only a country boy could know the real importance of April 15th.

I couldn't sleep last night. I never can sleep on the night before April 15th. For years I thought it was because of the pressure of work. There was always a trial waiting for me the next day. But judges and juries were not what I dreamed about the night before. I dreamed about home, about the mountains now awakening after a long winter's nap, about the early-morning chill in the air at this time of year, about the streams full of recently melted snow, and about the song sparrows who return in time to announce what every young boy in the country has waited for since Christmas: the first day of trout season.

The first day of trout season was always on April 15th in Pennsylvania. It was a school holiday. We were all so excited the day before, teachers and students alike, that nothing was done that did not involve the anticipation of what was to come the day after. Biology class was devoted to the study of trout, more important, their migratory habits in the nearby streams and, even more important, their eating habits on the following day. We talked about those we caught last year in History. And we measured them in Math. Of course, some students were hard to believe, but who were we to disbelieve the exploits of those whose success would undoubtedly be ours in another day?

Success does not come without planning, and I planned to be successful. That worried my father. It worried him because he was part of my plans. I planned to be on that stream by 3:30 A.M. so that we could get the best spot, which everyone in town knew about, and I was not about to let a reluctant father get in the way.

He tried! Every year it began the same way. Just after supper my mother would say, "I hope you fellows have a nice time tomorrow." The reason why she said that was because she knew we wouldn't. The reason why we wouldn't was because my father never wanted to get up until 5 A.M., even though the season began at 6 A.M. and

Country Living - April, Year Unknown

half the town was already on the stream by that time.

When I reminded my father of that fact, he always answered that the beauty in trout fishing was what you could see, not what you could catch, and no one could see anything in the dark. Now that made about as much sense to me as getting up at 5 A.M. The only things that I could see on that stream, when it grew light enough, were other trout fishermen, and I can't say that excited me very much. They were there to catch my fish, and I was not about to let that happen, even if it meant getting my father up at 3 A.M., just as I had every year since my mother decided that we should fish together on the first day.

My father did not take this lying down. In the first few years, he simply neglected to set the alarm and responded with disingenuous remorse when I became angry. The next year I set my own alarm only to find that he had locked his bedroom door. But that was not an insoluble problem to a boy from the country with a mission on his mind. I simply banged on the door until my mother woke up.

The rest was easy. Once awake, my father, now resigned, dressed and ate breakfast without so much as a comment. We were out of the house and on the stream in half an hour. Well, at least I was on the stream. My father stayed in the car, turned the heater on, and slept until daybreak.

Now, it is cold in those mountains at that time of year. It is even colder along the banks of a stream at 3:30 A.M. So you can imagine what it is like to stand in one, with water up to the top of your hip boots, waiting for the season to begin at day-break. The line would freeze in the eyelets of your fly rod. Your hands would become numb. You could no longer feel your toes after a while. But whatever discomfort I felt from all this did not compare to the embarrassment of watching my father sleep in that car. I could actually hear him snore over the roar of the stream. Well, anyway, I thought I could. Actually, it may have been one of the other fathers sleeping in one of the other cars.

I don't think that our fathers really ever understood how important the first day was to us. Failure to catch your "limit" could irreversibly affect the rest of your life. In fact, no young girl would ever marry someone who didn't; she knew, automatically, that he would be a failure at anything he did.

I have never failed to wake up exhausted on April 15th in recent years. Nor has the judge failed to notice it after I arrive in court. Last year, he asked me why I looked so tired. I told him I got up at 3 A.M. to go trout fishing. He looked at me in disbelief and then asked, "Why would anybody get up at 3 A.M. to go fishing?" I smiled, because he obviously had not grown up in the country, and answered, "to get a wife."

Real Men Don't See Doctors
Country Living's Healthy Living, Year Unknown

Real Men Don't See Doctors

More than nine million men have not had a medical checkup in the last five years. Why not? We asked lawyer Cal Golumbic—shameless advocate of the hedonistic life—to give us his views. Prepare to disagree!

"American women make 120 million more doctor visits per year than men," says Dr. Ken Goldberg in his book How Men Can Live as Long as Women (the Summit Group, $22.95). He also says that it's "not because they have more money or better insurance plans." Women, in his opinion, "are simply more attuned to taking care of themselves."

Great! It isn't enough that the medical profession is scaring the life out of women in this country. Now doctors are trying to do it to men. They say that we don't take care of ourselves. They've even done surveys to prove it. According to a recent survey conducted for Men's Health magazine and CNN, nearly 31 million, or about one-third of the nation's men, have not gone to the doctor for a medical checkup in a year. And more than nine million, or about one in 10, have not gone for a checkup in five years.

Well, why should they if there is nothing wrong with them? To begin with, people are supposed to go to doctors only when they're sick. Going to them when you're not is ridiculous. After all, do you go to an undertaker before you're dead? Now there's a logic you can't argue with. That's right, no matter what else you say about us, you have to acknowledge that men are logical—to the bitter end.

We're also cost-conscious, and if you doubt that, just look at one of those health-care surveys again. Yep, according to a survey of 1,500 physicians performed by the Men's Health Network, a nonprofit educational organization, men spend 50 percent less than women on health care.

Surprised? I'm not. Men know the value of a dollar. We're not about to go running to the doctor when we're not even sick. No, sir. We subscribe to that old adage that "a penny saved is a penny earned." We appreciate the need to invest for the long haul. We can see the big picture. That's right! Nobody can say that we're shortsighted.

That doesn't stop Dr. Goldberg,

Country Living's Healthy Living, Year Unknown

though. Nope, he doesn't like our attitude. He says that men are too competitive. Instead, they need to extend a helping hand to one another; they need to cooperate, talk honestly with one another, share feelings. Can you imagine? Maybe you can do those things in the medical profession, but you can't do them in my profession.

I'm a lawyer, a trial lawyer—I'm in the business of beating other lawyers. And I don't care how they feel about it. I don't care if they need help, either. You can be sure that I'm not about to help them or be any more honest with them than I have to. In fact, I don't know what cooperation means.

Dr. Goldberg says that it means men will live longer if they do it. Well, if I have to cooperate with the other side's lawyers, I don't want to live longer. Dr. Goldberg assures me that I and other men won't if we continue to eat the way we do. He says that we have got to stop eating red meat at all those power lunches. He also says that all those cream sauces, rich salad dressings, and sugary-sweet desserts have got to go.

Good lord. That's what guys eat! What's the matter with him? Doesn't he know that men are big, and we eat big, too? Yes, sir. We eat big steaks and big desserts, and we eat a lot of stuff that tastes good in between. That's why we call them power lunches—because they're powerfully good. And that's why we want to live a long time—so we can eat a lot. Yeah, it all comes down to logic. You can't separate men from logic. They go together, like a man and a big steak.

Dr. Goldberg says that men should go for fruit and vegetables, instead, especially those high in fiber. He wants men to eat whole-wheat bread, brown rice, apples, pasta, beans, carrots, oat bran, broccoli, prunes, and other high-fiber food. But that's what my wife eats! He wants me to eat women's food. I don't believe this; why should I eat that kind of food?

Because, Dr. Goldberg says, it is one of the reasons that women live an average of seven years longer than men. Uh...if they do, and they eat that stuff the whole time, all I can say is that they must be seven miserable years. But I don't really believe that diet is a reason why women live longer than men, anyway. No, women are just slower than men. Everyone knows that. Men simply finish living faster. That's not hard to understand, is it? It's just a matter of logic, again.

Apparently, Dr. Goldberg doesn't

understand logic, because even though men go through life a lot faster than women, he doesn't think that we exercise enough. Incredible, isn't it? I wonder what he thinks we do with our time. We're always on the go. That's because success is difficult. It's an uphill struggle: a climb that takes a lifetime. You don't think that we get there by sleeping, do you?

Oh, by the way, even while we're sleeping. we exercise. Sure, snoring really takes a lot of effort and every man snores; just ask his wife!

Evidently, that doesn't satisfy Dr. Goldberg. No, he says that we have to exercise while we're awake, too. Well, what do you call walking to the bank and to the restaurant every day? What do you call walking to the elevators and to the taxicabs every day? And I'm not even going to mention reaching across your desk to get the telephone about 20 times every day.

This is work, and work takes a lot out of you. I don't know how anyone can say otherwise. But we're not complaining; we're men. We know that we are not going to be here forever. So why not live while you can. You bet! Play hard and work hard; stop worrying; do everything in a big way; gamble it all. When you do that, you will feel like nothing can happen to you. You will feel like you're immortal. You will live forever—unless, of course, you get sick. and I don't know what you can do about that.

Lessons Learned
November 1989

Lessons Learned

In the country, fall foliage is an important ingredient in a well-known rite of passage.

It was late now. The office was nearly empty. It was time to go home. Out-side, the air was crisp. It is always that way in the fall, even in the city. The sun was rapidly setting in the west, but enough light remained to see the brilliant display of color in the leaves on the sugar maples lining the streets.

I never mind waiting on the corner for my next-door neighbor to pick me up at this time of year. I nearly forget from one year to the next just how beautiful a simple green maple leaf can become in the autumn. My neighbor, on the other hand, has a different view of leaves, especially when they have fallen in his front yard and are capable of being raked. He mentioned that view to me as we passed several front yards, not unlike his, which were also capable of being raked. But he saved his real wrath for the men who had, unlike himself, already raked their leaves into neat little piles. Not wanting to take issue with a job already done, or, in his case, yet to be done, he ignored the raking, both his and theirs, and condemned the burning of those nicely raked piles.

"A violation of the fire ordinance," he said, "and a public nuisance, to boot." His comment did not seem inappropriate here in the city, where everything, unregulated, is capable of becoming a nuisance, and some things, unsupervised, are capable of catching fire. In the country, however, most things tend to go unsupervised and unregulated. So learning is often based on day-to-day experience. And, in the case of boys, the experience includes the burning of leaves—in a corncob pipe.

When I spoke about the educational value of this experience, my neighbor listened quietly and continued to watch his urban counterparts rake their leaves into meaningless little piles in their front yards. Without taking his eyes off them, he said that I and those like me who find any value, let

Country Living - November 1989

alone educational value, in burning leaves in a corncob pipe must be out of our minds. Realizing that an educational practice was being questioned, I decided to defend it.

"Without smoking leaves in a corncob pipe, young boys in the country would never discover the principles fundamental to life or, at least, to a good life," I said. I didn't feel it necessary to point out that young girls discover these principles without ever engaging in such distasteful practices. I guess they learn from watching young boys. They were not about to get as sick as we got from things that we did, such as smoking a corncob pipe. This is easily explained: Little boys had fallen so far from God's grace that they had to suffer the consequences in order to discover that fact. Little girls, who had not fallen nearly so far, were merely required to watch them do it. They, as we all knew, learned far more easily or, at least, less painfully. How do I know these things? From smoking a corncob pipe.

But you learn other things, too. You learn how strong your father really is because he also did it-and survived. You learn how wise your mother is because she told you not to do it—and was right. You learn that there is a place for everything—in this case, behind the barn. And you learn that somebody will join you in nearly anything, even smoking leaves stuffed into a corncob pipe.

Of course, there are higher lessons to be learned. No one escapes easily from doing wrong; just ask a young boy the day after he's smoked that corncob pipe. And there is redemption, too. Ask him about that on the following day, when he can eat again. And ask him whether any young woman worth anything would ever marry a man who never smoked a corncob pipe behind the barn. The answer is no, for obvious reasons.

My neighbor, who by now had stopped watching his neighbors rake their leaves into nice little piles, asked, "Where did you ever learn such crazy things ?" I answered, simply, "In the country, behind a barn, smoking a corncob pipe."

A Halloween Horror
October 1990

A Halloween Horror

How Pastor Fleming met a headless horseman and took a cold bath.

Whenever I think of Halloween, I think about my mother's uncle—John Grove.

John Grove lived in a small farming village called Lemont, in central Pennsylvania. He was a farmer by trade and a Pennsylvania Dutch one at that. Like any Pennsylvania Dutch farmer, he was hardworking, stubborn, and mischievous, sometimes all at the same time. Recognizing that fact, I mean all at the same time, a Pennsylvania Dutch girl named Hannah Behrer consented to marry him. She, like any real Pennsylvania Dutch girl, could not resist the opportunity to temper the work, control the stubbornness, and eliminate the mischief. Unfortunately, although she was somewhat successful with respect to the work and the stubbornness, the mischief was unconquerable—especially on Halloween.

How do I know these things? My mother, another Pennsylvania Dutch woman, told me. And so did the storytellers in Lemont.

They recall the time when John Grove saddled a black stallion at about nine o'clock in the evening on Halloween and walked the horse down the yard and up onto the side porch of the house, where he mounted him. Dressed all in black, John Grove held a bucket of water in each hand. His turtleneck was pulled up over his head so that it looked like he didn't have one—only a big floppy hat on top of his shoulders. It was nearly dark now—just about time for the first Halloweeners to set foot on the front porch. Unfortunately for Pastor Fleming, but fortunately for the storytellers in Lemont, his were the first feet to set foot on John Grove's porch that night. Oblivious to the horror stories of those in years past who had dared to "hit" John Grove's house on Halloween night, Pastor Fleming had decided to do just that, except that his intentions were more noble.

Well, no matter what the intentions—as everyone in Lemont well knew, except, apparently, Pastor Fleming—no one was safe on John Grove's front porch on Halloween night-not even Pastor Fleming, or, rather, on this particular night, especially Pastor Fleming. John Grove, as the storytellers say, came down that side porch at a full gallop. My mother, who has always been too concerned with the truth to be a good storyteller, says that the horse walked down the side porch. Being a far better storyteller than my mother—because of less concern with the truth—I prefer to believe that he came at a gallop.

In any event, there is no dispute about what happened next. John Grove, astride that great horse, came around the corner of the house and into plain view of Pastor Fleming, screaming at the top of his lungs. Then, bearing down on the poor man, he rose in his stirrups, so that he stood at his full six-foot height, and raised both buckets of water over his head. Pastor Fleming, known more for his faith than his courage, by now had fallen to his knees and raised his arms over his head—according to the storytellers, to ask the Almighty to defend him. My mother, concerned as always with accuracy, says that it was to defend himself-from the inevitable drenching that followed.

Whatever the case, the only defense that Pastor Fleming received that night came from within, not from above. My mother's aunt, alarmed by the racket and quite aware of what her husband was capable of doing, especially on Halloween, opened the door somewhat apprehensively. To her horror, she discovered Pastor Fleming kneeling on the porch in front of the door, soaking wet and trembling, with a dark headless form—that she, unlike Pastor Fleming, quickly recognized as her husband—mounted on a black stallion. It was an ungodly sight—except for, of course, Pastor Fleming.

By that time, the storytellers say, Pastor Fleming had reached the fourth verse of the Twenty-Third Psalm—you know, the one that says, "Yea, though I walk through the valley of the shadow of death..." My mother, who has been the death of many a good story, says that the pastor couldn't speak. John Grove could, though. Realizing by now that any chance of everlasting life was in serious jeopardy, he said, without blinking an eye, "Hannah, where's your manners? Invite Pastor Fleming in for some hot cider!"

Saturday Night
May 1991

Saturday Night

In towns across America, the mating ritual continues.

It's Saturday night. Nothing special in the city—really. Only difference is that you don't have to work all day—usually. But the night is the same; just the obligations are different. They're social. Usually go to someone's house for dinner.

It wasn't always like that—not in the country, anyway. There, it was a special night—especially when you're young.

We talked about nothing else all Friday afternoon in high school. Before classes ended and the bell signaled the end of another week, we had planned what we were going to do beforehand, whom we would do it with, whose car we were going in, and whom we would take home afterward. But we didn't need to plan what we would do during Saturday night—at least not from nine to midnight, anyway. We did the same thing that our parents did before us: We went to the dance at the YMCA.

It was not just any dance—it was the dance. If one were not careful during the course of the evening, one could conceivably miss the girl of his dreams and any hope of marriage thereafter. Your fate, not to mention that of your unborn children, hung in the balance.

We were not unmindful of that fact as we approached the entrance, and entered accordingly. It was a serious moment and we masked that fact with a smile, much like one does at a funeral. After all, our social lives were at stake, and we knew it.

Danger was everywhere—dressed in long plaid skirts, penny loafers, bobby socks, and monogrammed sweaters. The sweaters, socks, loafers, and skirts joined others like them at one end of the gym—now turned dance—floor. It was a terrifying sight. There were so many of them and they were so self-confident—at least they seemed to be. What's more, you knew that they knew that you weren't. The only reason you stayed was because everyone else did and, of course, because your parents did and their parents before them, and, finally, because you had some debt to the human family or, at least, your family.

We sought refuge on the other side. Milling around uneasily, which is what herd animals do to avoid confronting predators one-on-one, we talked about nothing significant and everything insignificant, which is what high-school boys do to avoid confronting high-school girls one-on-one.

Every boy automatically became a friend, whether he was or not, because, with a little luck, we could all blend together and become indistinguishable—which we were: We all wore button-down shirts, khaki pants or jeans, and argyle socks. And every one of us had a crew cut, walked around in white buck shoes, and chewed gum—noisily.

But it didn't stop there. Oh, no! There was a characteristic swagger in our walk, an arrogance in our smile, and a general disdain for all things human—except, possibly, those things on the other side of the dance floor, which, by the way, were not—at least in our minds—so human.

Nevertheless, we were collectively—a force to be reckoned with. After all, hadn't we sent the vaunted Red Raiders back to Bellefonte all "black and blue" at the game last night? And wouldn't we end the season undefeated—for the first time in 20 years? Oh, yes! We were something else. We knew it; the school knew it; the town knew it; everyone knew it. Well—maybe not everyone on the other side of the dance floor.

But whatever security was gained from our collective conscious would be soon lost when the jukebox played the first song and we had to dance. Of course, this required crossing to the other side all by yourself.

It was a long and lonely walk. You could hear the taunts of those left behind, who by now were no longer your friends, sure that rejection and humiliation awaited you. It was only a question of by whom. Unfortunately, that question would be answered soon enough.

You could see the girls now quite clearly. They were armed with jewelry, borrowed in all likelihood from their older sisters, fortified in perfume, which their mothers no longer wanted, carried their provisions in handbags, and camouflaged their intentions—to reject and humiliate any young boy who happened along, behind a façade of makeup.

I approached their leader—and certain death—who was talking at the time—in all likelihood about whether to torture me or simply end it quickly. I stood behind her for about 20—no 30—years, until she finished. When she and her friends turned to look at me, now no more than six shaking inches high, I said, in a voice that barely could be heard, "Do you want to dance?"

To my amazement, she smiled, took my arm, and walked toward the dance floor. Then, when the music began, she turned, looked up at me, because I had grown 40 feet in the interval, and said, "Sure. Why not? It's Saturday night!"

The Girl Next Door
September 1991

The Girl Next Door

What do you do when you like someone so much you don't like them?

When I was young, I lived next door to Emilie Ann Hayes. I lived next door to her sister, Ruthie, too; but that was different. I liked Ruthie.

So did everyone else for that matter. Actually, they liked Emilie Ann, too. But just because someone is a good student; always, I mean always, cleans up his or her room; takes out the garbage without ever being asked, not once, mind you; never, no, not ever, gets in trouble; and likes everyone, even you—that is no reason to like them.

Everyone, however, was blinded by that smile. And they couldn't see past those bangs and that pert little nose.

Well, I could. After all, I had a better perspective. I had to live with all that every day. I mean, how would you like to be measured by someone like that who managed to get that way by the time she got to be your age. Yes, that's right, my age. And, what's more, I had to look up at her: She was at least six inches taller than me. A girl—and she was at least six inches taller than me.

It was really more than I could stand. Fortunately, Emilie Ann's father must have realized that, because he got a job in Williamsport, Pa., and took everything in the house with him, including Emilie Ann.

Things improved immediately. I managed to graduate from junior high school and to enter the tenth grade without a problem. The only problem in my life had packed up and gone to Williamsport with her family.

The problem reappeared, however, one week before the sophomore hop. It reappeared because, like all the other boys in the tenth grade, I hated dances, although not necessarily those with whom one had to dance.

So I refused to go. I say refused

because my mother insisted that I go, even though she knew that the sophomore hop was on April 15th—the first day of trout season. Mothers in central Pennsylvania never did understand the significance of the first day of trout season.

Realizing that I was in danger of having to go to the dance, I announced that it was too late to get a date. To my horror, my mother called Mrs. Hayes to see if Emilie Ann would go. To my amazement, Emilie Ann called back and said she would. Great. Can you imagine? Going with Emilie Ann Hayes to the sophomore hop on the first day of trout season, no less.

Emilie Ann and her folks appeared at our front door on the night of the dance. Of course, she was smiling. She was smiling because she had grown into a beautiful young lady and because she had grown more than I had. Both reasons were enough to ruin what already promised to be a disastrous evening.

I gave her the corsage that my mother had made and she thanked me and, of course, smiled. We danced the first and last dance, like you're supposed to, and I didn't see much of her in between. At the end of the evening, we drove home where her folks were waiting to take her back to Williamsport. She stood with them at the door, smiling, and thanked everyone for such a nice evening. And then she was gone. So, too, was the smile. I wouldn't see either for 30 years.

Apparently, she married a naval officer, adopted two children, and lived over the years at a number of bases across the country. Everyone, they say, now calls her Ann.

Last fall, my mother told me that Emilie Ann's husband had retired from the service and that they had bought a farm just outside a little town near Williamsport. "Why don't you call her?" Mother said. It didn't take me long to think of several reasons why, but my mother was persistent and I finally did several days later.

We talked for a long time about everything without really saying anything. I was polite; she was warm and gracious. The conversation ended when she asked me to visit them on Sunday. I politely refused; she warmly insisted. And, for reasons that I do not understand—even now—I finally agreed.

Emilie Ann opened the front door. She was smiling. After introducing me to her husband, she took me on a tour of their house, followed by a tour of their farm. Then we all sat down in the living room and talked.

It was not difficult to remember why everyone always liked her. She laughed about Ruthie, who had married a rancher in Montana. She worried a little bit, like all mothers, about her children.

There was concern in her voice when she spoke about her parents. And there was devotion in her eyes when she looked at her husband.

She served us sandwiches and tomato soup, which is what girls often serve their fellows for lunch in central Pennsylvania. Her husband said that she was a great cook and it didn't take me long to agree.

We talked for much of the meal about our childhood. Emilie Ann remembered some things about mine that now seemed really funny. And we all laughed about them. I can't remember ever having more fun with anyone.

When we finished, I thanked them both for lunch and said that I must be going. Her husband shook hands with me at the door and Emilie Ann walked with me to the car. When we got there, she turned, looked at me, and asked: "Will we ever see you again?" I smiled politely because that's the most that boys from central Pennsylvania can do in circumstances like that.

As I drove away, I looked at her briefly in the rearview mirror. She was smiling. And I realized for the first time that I liked Emilie Ann Hayes.

"Amazing," I said to myself, "how much people change. Emilie Ann, I mean."

Raising Your Parents
February 1992

Raising Your Parents

It was tough work teaching Mom and Dad
to control themselves.

People, nowadays, are always worried about kids. They say it's impossible to raise them in a world like this. Well, I don't know much about the world we live in now, but I knew something about the one I grew up the one I grew up in a long time ago in central PA ago central Pennsylvania. The problem then was not raising kids. No, sir! The problem was raising parents.

It wasn't easy. After all, you couldn't let them know you were doing it. Otherwise, it just wouldn't work. Parents had all that pride and not too much knowledge to go with it. Oh, they could add and subtract all right, but they didn't know much about kids.

Why else would they talk like that when we were babies? You couldn't even understand them. And they did it in front of other people, too. If it had been just my mother, it might not have been so bad. But my dad did it once, too—right in front of the guys at the Kiwanis Club's annual family picnic.

It was in the bottom of the ninth inning of the annual softball game with the Kiwanis Club from Bellefonte. All of the wives from both teams were watching. More was at stake here than a win. My mother held me up so that my dad could see me just as somebody hit a pop fly to him at first base. My dad saw me, but not the pop fly; he was too busy talking to me. And, to make matters worse, he started talking like that. Yeah... like that.

Well, Dad missed the pop fly. I threw up on Mrs. Himes. Bellefonte scored two more runs in the bottom of the ninth. And we lost the game.

How do you expect to win in life when your first baseman acts like that? The only one who ever forgot about the whole sorry mess was Mrs. Himes. Thank God she did. Mrs. Himes turned out to be my first-grade teacher. I didn't know it at the time, so I couldn't wait to start school. My parents, however, were quite another matter.

Before that first day of school, Mother bawled all night. Can you imagine? The

Country Living - February 1992 35

whole night! How would you like to go to school on the first day without any sleep? Actually, now that I think about it, I was lucky to get there at all. My mother came in to wake me up and started hugging me. And she wouldn't let go. Finally, I told her to get control of herself, which worked about as long as it took me to get dressed. Then the whole thing started all over again.

In desperation, I called to my dad. Boy, was that a mistake! He tried to kiss me. He hadn't tried anything like that since the Kiwanis Club picnic. And I told him about it. Apparently, it had some effect because only my mother insisted on walking me to school.

Dad, however, insisted on teaching me to drive when I turned 16. He did so because everyone knew that he was a better driver than my mother. Well, at least my dad knew. Confident in that knowledge, Dad drove me all around town. Then he suggested that I try it myself—with the instruction that I just follow his driving techniques.

Well, I did. I blew the horn at a neighbor, as he was backing out of his driveway, because, as my father says, he never watched what he was doing. Then I passed another neighbor because, as usual, she was going too slow, and raced to make the yellow light at Third and Main. I made it just as the light turned red. Well—maybe just after it turned red. Hey! This was my first trip.

Dad was disgusted. He said that I had learned absolutely nothing and that I was a menace to everything on the road. Gosh, I didn't know how he could say that. I wondered where I had gone wrong in life.

I wasn't wrong, however, about girls. Oh, no! I liked them right from the start. You just knew that they were going to be important some day. You also knew that your parents were pretty uptight about the whole thing. So I just said that I didn't like them. That seemed to work pretty well.

At least it did until the sophomore hop. It was on the first day of trout season and I had planned to go fishing. But Mother had a fit, so I had to forget about fishing and go to the dance. Gee, I wonder what changed!

Whatever it was, I decided not to oppose it. So, one year later, I asked Hellen Ann Shaffer if I could walk her home after the dance at the Y on Saturday night. My parents simply got quiet when I told them. But they went absolutely berserk when I explained that Hellen Ann had invited me in to make popcorn the following week and her parents weren't home. You'd think she was going to poison me or something!

It isn't easy having parents. You never know what will set them off next. Of course, it's a little different with my kids. They would be the first to tell you how much they've profited from my central-Pennsylvania ways. Unfortunately, you can't ask them right now. My older son went off to live in Austin, Texas. And my younger son went off to school in Chicago. I never could understand why they didn't want to stay in Washington, D.C., with their old dad.

Pontiac Madness
June 1992

Pontiac Madness

The muffler was gone and the brakes were a big sluggish, but our 1929 convertible made high school a time to remember.

Kids nowadays really aren't like we were growing up in the country. They don't seem to have any spunk. Halloween is nothing more than a trip next door to say "trick or treat." And, they go to school without so much as a squack. Sunday school is fun. Can you imagine! Sure, these things are important. My mother says you can't get to heaven without 'em. Well, that's probably true. But, as they say in central Pennsylvania, where I grew up, most boys raise a little hell on the way.

In our case, we did it in a red-and-black 1929 Pontiac convertible. It was a great car. There wasn't another one like it in the whole state of Pennsylvania. The body was sleek with good lines and low to the ground like a greyhound running hard in full stride. The wheels were big and durable with spokes like those on a Roman chariot. And the engine was a thing of beauty even after two decades of use and, probably, some misuse.

God saw fit to leave only a couple of these mechanical creations on earth by the time we got to high school. And, in His infinite wisdom, He put one of them in our hands. Unfortunately, the one we got didn't have a muffler, as anyone over in Centre County could tell you, and it didn't have a top at least one that you could put up, anyway.

It did have brakes, however, no matter what anyone says to the contrary. Sure, they didn't work like the ones you have now; they were mechanical. You had to pump them 60 or 70 times and then pull on the emergency brake. After that, it was usually no more than 100 yards or so before the car would stop.

Of course, on those occasions when the car did not stop within 100 yards, it caused some problems. Once, we ran over a rooster when we alertly pulled into a cornfield just before the steep grade running down into Bellefonte. I don't know why the farmer got so mad. The rooster was mean as dirt and the farmer probably had him for dinner anyway. And, if we had gone down that grade, the damage to Bellefonte would have exceeded that caused by our football team, which soundly trounced theirs that year.

Usually, however, it was just a question of trying to find some place to steer the car at an intersection full of cars waiting for the light to change. It required some real imagination on occasion. Apparently, the drivers of the cars waiting for the light to change did not have any imagination because they reacted accordingly. Actually, now that I think of it, some of their reactions were a little dramatic. I mean, why drive off the Jay Street bridge when any reasonable person could see that we were going to turn at the last moment to avoid a collision? And can you imagine telling the police, afterward, that it was better to take your chances in the river than be "disabled for the rest of your life by that contraption"?

It wouldn't have been so bad if the local newspaper hadn't picked up the story. I think that's what caused all the hysteria that followed. We couldn't approach an intersection with cars waiting for the light to change without drivers panicking. And, to make matters worse, we became the subject of a sermon on the "power of prayer" over at Great Island Presbyterian Church and one week later the "prodigal son" apparently returned over at Trinity Methodist Church in a red-and-black 1929 Pontiac convertible.

Frankly, I think it was a little presumptuous of the flock over at Trinity to think that we were ready to return to the fold, which, by the way, we eventually did, but not before stopping a few times at the Star Lite Drive-In Theater just outside of Mill Hall. Now, I don't think it's so unusual for a couple of high-school boys to spend an evening at a drive-in theater, no matter how bad the movie, when they're going with the best-looking girls in the senior class. But it is when you can't get the top to go up in the car. I don't think there was a mosquito in central Pennsylvania that didn't know our blood types. And it wasn't much better in the winter. There's no cold like being cold in an open car in a drive-in in central Pennsylvania.

Well, we were not without solutions. We kept two heavily worn deerskin blankets in the trunk for

ILLUSTRATION BY JAMES A. WILLIS

such occasions in the winter and a can of Ole Moose insect repellent in the summer. The difficulty, of course, was cuddling up with someone who smelled like a moose in the summer and who looked like one in the winter.

I can't remember what ever happened to the car. Funny, since it was such an important part of my life. I guess it just got left behind somewhere in central Pennsylvania. Or, maybe, like the rest of my childhood, it became a part of me and made me what I am—just a country boy.

The Lemont Band Hall
July 1992

The Lemont Band Hall

In central Pennsylvania, the routine of daily life was broken only on Monday nights.

My mother grew up in a sleepy little farming village in central Pennsylvania. It was situated at the foot of Mount Nitany, where the Nitany (mountain) lion roamed—when it wasn't attending class at Penn State just a few miles away. The name of the village was Lemont, which in French means "the mount," in obvious recognition of the mountain that towers above it. Why it was given a French name is more difficult to explain because nearly all of its inhabitants were Pennsylvania German. They numbered about 200 if you didn't count in August, when most of them were over at the Grange fair in Centre Hall.

Now, routine was important to the Pennsylvania German farmers in Lemont. They usually got up with the chickens, as they were apt to say, and, after finishing a hearty breakfast, worked, except for a brief interruption at lunchtime, until dinner, which was served about 5:00 P.M., so when they finished dinner, they would sit on the front porch until bedtime, which, of course, was early so that they could get up at the same time the next morning and do the same things all over again. This routine was broken only on Monday evenings in Lemont. That was when the band practiced in the Lemont band hall.

Everyone in Lemont would sit on his front porch and listen. You could hear the band practice all the way up and down Branch Road because they always left the front door of the band hall open. My mother says they did that because there were too many of them to fit into the tiny little band hall. The old men in Lemont, however, say it was because, after the first two numbers, the place smelled like a cattle barn. My mother says that wasn't true because the band members always changed their work clothes before coming to practice. The old men in Lemont,

Country Living - July 1992

however, say that didn't make any difference.

It was always interesting to see where everyone in the band sat, which, like everything else in central Pennsylvania, never changed from week to week. The tuba player always sat by the front door. The reason he always sat by the front door, my mother says, was because he always helped his wife do the dishes before coming to band practice, and therefore was always late. The old men in Lemont, however, say that he was always late because he was not a Pennsylvania German farmer, and if you're not a Pennsylvania German farmer the chances are you're always going to be late. My mother responded that if you are a Pennsylvania German farmer the chances are that you're not going to help your wife do the dishes.

The trombone player always sat a little bit away from everyone else. My mother says this was because he was a music major "up at the college," and he really didn't know the other members of the band very well. The old men in Lemont, however, say it was because he was the only one in the whole band who could play worth anything and he was embarrassed to sit with the rest of them.

The fellows in the trumpet section always sat in the back of the room. They were all from Houserville, which is just on the other side of Puddintown. The old men in Lemont say that the reason they always sat in the back was because the fellows from Puddintown, who all played the clarinet, always sat in the front. Apparently, the old men in Lemont say, someone from Puddintown sneaked over to Houserville one night and caught that big brown trout that the fellows from Houserville had been trying to catch for years. It caused some pretty hard feelings, the old men in Lemont say.

Well, I won't dispute that there were some pretty hard feelings; but, in my opinion, what really happened was that the trout died of old age. I mean, the fellows from Houserville had been trying to catch that trout for years, and a trout, like a good story, can't last forever. My mother, who has heard the story, just says that you should be able to expect more from grown men. The old men in Lemont, however, say that they had better not catch anyone from Puddintown fishing anywhere near Lemont.

You can't hear the band practice anymore on Monday evenings in Lemont. The band disbanded many years ago. The band hall still stands where it used to, but now it's called the Art Alliance, and it serves as a studio for artists.

The old men in Lemont say that it's the first time that any art has ever come out of that building. My mother just smiles and says that it's the first time that the men in Lemont were ever interested in art. Actually, my mother is wrong there. I remember the time when there was a nude painting in an art exhibit up at the college.

My Best Friend
February 1993

My Best Friend

What do you do when your pal is the best-looking, smartest, and nicest guy in the class?

Everybody has a best friend while he grows up. I don't know why. It is one of those things that is hard to explain. I don't even know if I can explain what a best friend is. I just know that I had one. His name was Steve Romeo.

Steve lived in a duplex up on South High Street with his dad, mom, and one sister. He was taller than I was, with dark eyes and dark hair. All the girls said that he was one of the best-looking guys in the class. He was also one of the best athletes. No one did better academically; everyone liked him; and he really was a nice guy.

I guess it was that last quality—being so nice, I mean—that was so irritating.

When you are trying to do better than someone else—because he is your best friend—the last thing in the world that you need is to have him be nice about it.

Take, for example, the time we both made the Little League all-star baseball team. And our coach decided to use us as pitchers. Well, he also decided to use Steve as a pitcher in the national championship game against Pensacola, Fla. I, on the other hand, was put in the outfield—for the whole game. You couldn't even see me out there. And no one even hit one out of the infield. I didn't do much more at the plate either: struck out four times. Steve pitched a shutout, and the team gave him the ball at the end of the championship.

If that was not bad enough, Steve had everyone on the team sign the ball and then he gave it to me for Christmas. The card on the front of the box said, "For the best player on the team from your best friend, Steve." That was the trouble. He was, and I wasn't: He was my best friend, and I wasn't the best player on the team. He was. To make matters worse, he was so nice about it.

Steve was the same way about girls. Of course, he was going steady with Marilyn Dumm, who was the

Country boy Cal Golumbic and best friend Steve Romeo (the taller, better-looking guy on the right) at their graduation from Lock Haven High School in 1954.

Country Living - February 1993

53

best-looking girl our age in the whole universe. I, on the other hand, was still hoping that I might grow taller than some girl our age in the whole universe. And, of course, my size, or lack of it, made the dance every Saturday night at the YMCA a miserable affair.

No girl in her right mind wants to dance with a boy who is shorter than she is. So, when it was "lady's choice," which must have been every minute and a half, the only girls who ever asked me to dance were Marilyn's best friends. The only reason they asked me to dance was because Marilyn asked them to. And the only reason Marilyn asked them to was because Steve asked her to. I mean everybody in school knew that. It was so humiliating.

So was being Steve's campaign manager for president of the senior class. Naturally, he was nominated—by about everybody in the class. I was, too—by Steve. Well, in a runoff election to determine our party's candidate, Steve won by a landslide. How much of a landslide? I think that the only one who voted for me was Steve.

To make matters worse, right afterward Steve appointed me his campaign manager. Can you imagine? Now I had to help him win. Well, he did and when he walked up on the stage in the school auditorium to a standing ovation by the whole school—teachers, too—you will never believe what he said. Oh, sure, he thanked everybody and said a few other things that nobody will ever remember. But right after that, he just stood there for a few moments until the auditorium grew quiet, then he began to speak again, only this time in a more serious manner.

Steve said that there was someone who really was responsible for all this and that he wanted him to come up there on the stage with him. "You all know him," he said. "He is as much your friend as he is mine." I couldn't hear the rest; the noise of everybody applauding was too loud. But I could see Steve pointing to me and I could see everyone around motioning me to get up. I did and I walked up there and stood beside him on the stage. I can't tell you for how long. I guess it was a lifetime.

I was so proud. I am not sure why. Maybe it was because we won the election; maybe it was because I was up there on that stage; or maybe it was because Steve Romeo was my best friend. I guess the only thing that I am sure about, now that I think about it, is that I know what a best friend is: A best friend is somebody you like even though you don't.

The Wirehaired Terror
June 1993

The Wirehaired Terror

The two-sided tale of a dog named Binky.

My mother was raised by her Aunt Hannah and Uncle John Grove in a small Pennsylvania German farming community called Lemont, which is located in Centre County. Now the Pennsylvania Germans were some of the finest farmers in the world, but they could also be some of the most difficult. And those who lived in Lemont were no exception. None, however, were more difficult than the men of the Grove family. They were, according to the old men in Lemont, "absolutely impossible" especially my mother's Uncle John. But even he, according to the old men in Lemont, paled in comparison to Binky Grove, who was, so their story goes, as mean as the tomcat over at the next town, Oak Hall.

My mother, who absolutely adored Binky—her little wirehaired terrier—said that the old men in Lemont were not fair and that, with the possible exception of the old men in Lemont, Binky loved all creatures on this earth, two- and four-legged alike.

Oh yeah, countered the old men in Lemont, what about the time that Binky jumped out of the window of my mother's model T Ford while she was driving over by Pleasant Gap and ran after Burlin Chilcoat's prize bull, which he had just let out of the barn.

Binky, my mother corrected, accidentally fell out of the window. Then, according to my mother, Binky became disoriented when he hit his head on the road and wandered too close to the bull, who, for no reason other than being meanspirited, attacked poor Binky.

The bull attacked Binky, the old men in Lemont responded, because he had already sunk his teeth two inches into the bull's leg, only after, by the way, leaping out of the window the moment he saw him. According to the old men in Lemont, it took Burlin and two of his field hands 10 minutes to pry that dog off of that bull.

My mother insisted that that was preposterous. Binky, she stated, let go of the bull as soon as she parked the car, walked out into the field, and told him to. Binky, she added, was a very well-behaved dog; everyone knows that. Why, my mother went on, there isn't a person in Lemont who doesn't know about the time that she took Binky with her on a trip to the Roxy theater in Lock Haven to see a Western. Because it was too hot to leave him in the car, she asked the girl at the ticket booth if she could take Binky into the theater. Since the girl could easily see how well behaved Binky was, my mother continued, the girl agreed on the condition that my mother keep him on the seat beside her. And, my mother concluded, that's just where Binky stayed.

He stayed there, said the old men in Lemont, until the movie began and Roy Rogers rode into view. Then, in the blink of an eye, he leaped off his seat, tore down the aisle, and put a two-inch gash in Trigger's leg—or the Roxy's movie screen, whichever way you prefer to look at it. Since the owners of the Roxy preferred to look at their movie screen, or rather the two-inch gash in it, the old men in Lemont continued, my mother and the creature who bit Trigger in the leg were invited to leave.

My mother acknowledged that she and Binky were asked to leave; but, she explained, that was only because the owners did not know about the time that poor Binky was maliciously attacked by Burlin Chilcoat's bull, and that Binky was notoriously nearsighted and had simply mistaken Roy Rogers's horse, Trigger, for Burlin Chilcoat's bull.

The old men in Lemont asked my mother if Binky had mistaken my father for Burlin Chilcoat's bull when he tore the seat out of my father's pants as he walked up the steps of the front porch to pick up my mother for their first date.

That was a completely different situation, my mother answered; after all, my father had been a stranger to Binky, and like most males in Lemont, Binky did not particularly care for strangers. To make matters worse, my mother went on, my father had passed through Oak Hall on his way over, and Binky, seeing the car coming from that direction, was sure that my father was from Oak Hall.

Binky and 18-month-old Cal Golumbic play ball at Aunt Hannah's.

Now that explanation did not seem unreasonable to the old men in Lemont. My mother was right: If there was one thing they did not like, it was strangers, especially if the strangers were from Oak Hall. Apart from a long-standing rivalry, which had its origins in a loss in the tractor pull at the Grange Fair in Centre Hall in 1897, the tomcat over at Oak Hall had been terrorizing everyone in Lemont for years.

In any event, despite what was admitted to be a reasonable explanation for the hole in the seat of my father's pants, the old men in Lemont suggested that the whole incident must have been embarrassing to my mother. She answered that the only incident that ever embarrassed her occurred when Binky picked a fight with the tomcat over at Oak Hall.

I asked my mother why Binky's run-in with the tomcat had embarrassed her, and she answered that it was because the old men in Lemont blew the whole thing out of proportion.

"Did they really malign Binky?" I asked.

"No, just the opposite," she answered. "They tried to get him elected to County Council."

Capture The Flag
August 1993

Capture the Flag

Learning the rules of the game—and
how they change.

We played "capture the flag" every night the summer that I was 10. We played it in Price Park, which was two times the length of a football field and just about as wide, with nothing much in it except weeds and trees. Oh sure, there was grass, too, but the grass was never cut very often.

We didn't mind. The trees and the weeds and the tall grass made it easy to hide, and hiding was an important part of the game. It was important because if you were seen crossing the line that a streetlight made down the middle of the park, then the other team could capture you and imprison you at the base of the tree on which they'd hung their flag. Of course, if you didn't cross the line into their territory, you couldn't capture their flag.

With these rules in mind, I chose my team night after night. Rules were not, however, the only thing that I had in mind as I chose them. There were other consid-erations, too. Take Emilie Ann Hayes, for example. Emilie Ann was a girl; but that was only the half of it. She was also fast— and cunning, too. It was impossible to catch her.

It was also impossible to choose her first. Remember, she was a girl. A guy just couldn't choose a girl first. But you also knew that the other side couldn't either. No, they, like you, had to wait until it seemed like there was no other choice. Then you chose her reluctantly. You just made sure that you reluctantly did it before the other side had the chance to.

I mean, the only thing worse than having Emilie Ann Hayes on your team was having her on the other team. Can you imagine what it was like to be caught by a girl? If you can, then you can understand why I made sure that she was on our team.

Wally Smith was on our side, too, but for different reasons. In the first place, he was one of my best friends. A guy just had to take somebody like that. You just didn't have to take him in the first round. You didn't, because the other side wouldn't. They wouldn't because he was too slow. And in this game, slow was not an asset. You did not capture a flag slowly.

Of course, you couldn't capture

one if you were dumb either, and Wally Smith was not dumb. No sir. Wally was smart. He was certainly smart enough to know that he could not catch anyone on the other team. So I always chose him to stay back and guard our flag.

Now usually, everyone chooses a guy who is fast to stay back and guard the flag. That way, if someone sneaks through your lines in the darkness, the guy who stays back can catch him before he captures your flag. The only trouble is that, by the end of the game, three or four people usually wind up sneaking through your lines-and no matter how fast the guy is who stays back, he can't catch them all, not all at the same time, anyway.

Well, Wally couldn't catch anybody at any time. So he stood next to the tree where the flag was hanging and waited for one of them to get almost close enough to grab it. When he did, Wally captured and imprisoned him, making him stand at the base of the tree. The only way a prisoner could be freed was for one of his teammates to get close enough to touch him. And you know what that meant.

Then, of course, there was the Sport factor. Sport was Wally's springer spaniel, and everywhere that Wally went, Sport went, too— which meant that Sport never moved from the base of that tree, either. In fact, every time someone got within 30 feet of it, Sport would howl and point in that direction. This was not lost on the other team, and they complained bitterly. I guess they were bitter because I usually got Wally, and Sport, in the sixth or seventh round.

Getting Charlie Lair was a little bit trickier. Unlike Wally, Charlie was really fast so you couldn't let too many rounds go by without taking him or the other side would. You could usually wait until the fourth or fifth round, however, because everyone knew that even though Charlie was fast, he was always the first one to get caught.

The reason was obvious. Charlie's mother would not let him crawl on the ground like the rest of us did to avoid being seen crossing the line into the other side's territory. When you crawl on the ground you get dirty, and Charlie's mother did

Clean Charlie Lair, the team of Wally Smith and Sport, and their captain, Cal.

not like dirt. So Charlie always ran across the line to avoid getting dirty, not to avoid getting caught, which, in his mind, had less significant consequences.

Well, the consequences may have been less significant, but they were no less in-evitable. Charlie inevitably got caught before anyone else, which is why the other team was reluctant to choose him. That, however, was why I was reluctant not to choose him.

Getting caught early in the game could be helpful. Then, you would be imprisoned at the base of the tree where the other team's flag was hung and your team would know exactly where their flag was. Until then, it was impossible to tell in the darkness.

The other team never did understand this. In fact, they never understood how our team could win at all. I just said that things have a habit of working out.

Things also have a habit of changing. Take Price Park, for example. The weeds are gone, and they cut the grass now. There are recreational facilities, too. They even changed the name to Hanna Park. Emilie Ann Hayes got married and changed her name, too. Gosh, I don't think she even runs anymore. Wally Smith does, though; he runs five miles every evening. Even more amazing,

Charlie Lair became a painter and looks a mess every night when he gets home.

Yes, I guess that everything changes after a while. Well, maybe not everything. I became a lawyer.

My Education
October 1993

My Education

There was a lot a college student could learn from working at the Tavern.

I attended school at Penn State University's State College campus, but I got my education across the street at the Tavern. The Tavern was a restaurant with good food—and more. The good food was provided by the cooks; the "more" was provided by the two proprietors, John ("Jace") O'Connor and Ralph Yeager.

These were no ordinary men. Oh, no! They were two eccentric academics who decided not to pursue the careers in engineering and chemistry for which their respective educations had prepared them, but instead, to open a small restaurant for which nothing had prepared them.

They, of course, would never agree that they had come to the business unprepared. In endless lectures given to the young men who were unfortunate enough to be working their way through college by waiting tables at the Tavern, of which I was one, the owners explained that the way to prepare for anything you might do in the future was to do the very best you could at whatever it might be you were doing now so that the habits you gained from doing so would stay with you the rest of your life. Now, all that may have meant something to you when you were 20 years of age, but it didn't mean much to me. I didn't wait tables at the Tavern to gain any habits, good or bad. No, I waited on tables at the Tavern for a more practical reason: No other place in town paid as well.

Jace and Ralph believed that it was important to pay people well. It was part of that whole boring lecture thing. I never really did understand it—either the lectures or paying that well. But I was not about to complain—about being paid that well, I mean.

Oh, sure, we were required to "split tips," dividing the money evenly among all the waiters at the end of the evening. Jace and Ralph said that splitting tips fostered a sense of collegiality among the waiters and, of course, helped the younger ones until they could do as well as the rest of us. Oh, brother! There was nothing that I enjoyed more than splitting tips with some idiot who didn't know what he was doing his first day on the job.

The tips were good, though. You

couldn't complain about that. I guess it had a lot to do with the food, but it also had something to do with the way the food was served. You see, Jace and Ralph had this system: Every waiter was assigned a section, and when he took an order, he wrote the section number down on the order slip. He also wrote down the table number and the customers' orders, beginning with the person seated at the northern end of the table and then proceeding clockwise. That meant that when the food was prepared, it didn't have to sit on the serving table until the waiter assigned to that section got back to the kitchen to pick it up. Whoever happened to be in the kitchen at the time could take it out and serve the people at the table, who, of course, were absolutely amazed that this waiter knew who got what without having to ask.

Great! Leave it to an engineer and a chemist to mess things up. Because of their stupid system, I had to take care of everyone else's tables as well as my own.

Jace and Ralph said that helping others was an important thing to learn. Somehow it seemed that all the things that Jace and Ralph thought were important to learn involved a lot of work. Frankly, because of that, I didn't care whether I ever learned any of them.

I didn't care whether I ever learned about classical music, either, and that's all they ever played at the Tavern. No one under 25 liked classical music unless there was something the matter with him, and there was nothing the matter with me. That didn't make any difference to Jace and Ralph. They said that there was something noble about music that had survived for ages. Jace and Ralph were big on "noble."

They were also big on antiques, so there was no furniture in that restaurant except antiques. You always had to be careful not to set your tray on top of them. Antiques may not be very sturdy, but they are valuable.

Left: *Tavern owners Jace O'Connor and Ralph Yeager in 1975.* Below: *Waiting to be served food and advice, a hungry '50s crowd gathers at the Tavern.*

Jace and Ralph's collection of old prints alone was worth thousands.

I heard that sometime after I graduated from Penn State, Jace and Ralph donated some of those old prints to a museum at the college. Incredible! The only thing worthwhile about those prints was their value, and those guys gave them away. I never could understand those guys.

I never could understand why I had to serve dinner to the older waiters, either. It was another one of Jace and Ralph's crazy policies. They reserved a table in the dining room where the waiters could eat at the end of the evening. The waiters were allowed to have anything they liked except the most expensive items on the menu. I always understood the reason for that. Anyway, it really didn't matter, because all of the food was terrific, especially the cheesecake, which was Ralph's mother's recipe. Still, I didn't understand why I had to serve the older waiters. It was just more work, and they didn't tip.

Jace and Ralph said that having their dinner served was something the older waiters had earned and something the younger waiters could look forward to. Well, looking forward to it didn't do me much good because I graduated before I ever got the chance to be served.

Oh, by the way, I didn't give notice to my landlord until one week before graduation. He wasn't happy about it and told Jace so. Naturally, Jace was not happy about it, either, so he told me so in another lecture— about timeliness this time.

You can see why I didn't mind leaving the Tavern. Amazingly, some of the other waiters did, though. Two of them stayed on and helped manage the restaurant for more than 30 years. Two others bought the place a few years ago. I guess Jace and Ralph had some effect on those guys. Well, I can assure you that they didn't have any effect on me.

That's why I wrote this article.

The Christmas Gift
December 1993

The Christmas Gift

How a Pennsylvania German girl's love of music led to family harmony—and occasional discord.

My grandmother Anna Behrer was Pennsylvania German (which some people call Pennsylvania Dutch). She also happened to be a fine musician. Now that may not seem unusual to you, but that is probably because you are not Pennsylvania German. Pennsylvania Germans do not think very highly of frivolous things, and music is very high on their list of frivolous things. But Pennsylvania Germans are also independent, proud, and, on some occasions, stubborn, and my grandmother was more stubborn than most—a trait, I hear, with some disbelief, that continues in our family to this day. So, despite the disapproval of her entire family, which could be quite unrelenting, she persisted in pursuing her musical interests.

Actually, music became more than an interest after her husband died: It became the way by which she supported herself and her eight-year-old daughter. My grandmother became a music teacher—circuit style.

This meant that she had to travel by horse and buggy to farm villages all over Centre County, one after another. She would stay with a family that had a piano—giving the children free lessons—just long enough to accommodate all the families in the surrounding countryside who were interested in giving their children music lessons. Then, at the end of two weeks or so, she would return home.

Home was now with her sister, Hannah Behrer, who had married John Grove and who, with him, owned a farm in the village of Lemont. It was a perfect arrangement because the Groves did not have any children, except, some said, John Grove himself, and my grandmother needed someone to look after her daughter while she was away.

The Groves did just that. John, who was a typical Pennsylvania German farmer (which means that he was religious, industrious, and cantankerous, although not necessarily in that order), taught my mother that God forgave man, or at least the Pennsylvania German variety, even if he'd spent part of his week tormenting his niece and teasing his wife, so long as he worked hard the rest of the time and went to church on Sunday. Hannah, on the other hand, taught my mother that even if God did forgive such men, their wives, who had less patience, did not—which is why they tried to change them. At other times, Hannah taught my mother to sew, a skill which my mother has conveniently forgotten, and to cook, one which, thankfully, she has not.

Then, of course, there was that big old farmhouse. Despite having every other comfort, it did not have a piano. For a while, my mother practiced at the home of one of her friends, Jane Cowell, in State College. That posed a problem, however, because State College was nearly five miles away and my mother had to walk there. Consequently, she couldn't practice every day.

At first, the teacher would not take my mother as a student because she did not have a piano. But my mother, who is also Pennsylvania German and no less stub-born, convinced the teacher that it would not present a problem. That, however, was not the end of the matter. Now convinced that she needed a piano, my mother asked for one nearly every day for the next year.

Neither of the Groves was particularly pleased by this. It was not that they couldn't afford a piano; they simply did not want one. Hannah, because she dearly loved her niece, eventually gave in. John, however, did not—for the very same reason. In his opinion, spending $500 on a piano, which was what one cost in those days, was more than frivolous; it was corrupt, and he was not about to corrupt his only niece. And he told her so. My mother thought that this was ridiculous. And she told him so. And the debate went on like this day after day until, finally exasperated, John ended the conversation by telling my mother—and everyone else in Centre County—that the only way she would get a piano would be "over my dead body."

The purchase of a piano was never discussed again.

John and Hannah Grove owned a farm in the Pennsylvania village of Lemont.

Pennsylvania Germans, besides being stubborn, are also forgiving, especially with those they love, and uncle, aunt, and niece loved each other. So they resumed their lives accordingly and enjoyed one another's company, despite the teasing and tormenting, until John Grove fell ill with tuberculosis two years later. He was subsequently hospitalized, became progressively worse, despite daily visits by his wife and niece, and died just after Thanksgiving.

Christmas would not be the same that year. Nevertheless, my mother and her aunt joined together on Christmas Morning to exchange gifts under the tree as they always had. When all the gifts were unwrapped, my mother's aunt handed her a small package. It was from her uncle John. My mother opened the package and found a page from his will. Underlined were the following words: "I bequeath $500 to my beloved niece for a piano." My mother looked up and, with tears in her eyes, said, "I don't understand." Her aunt smiled and said softly, "He was a man of his word."

Almost Heaven
February 1994

Almost Heaven

Some folks don't realize that you don't have to die to find heaven.

Everyone is always so concerned about Heaven. They spend half their time wondering about what it is like. And you hear endless opinions on the subject. Well, I can tell you, they're all wrong.

For starters, heaven's streets are certainly not paved with gold. The state would never appropriate enough money for that. Heck, it takes an act of God to get the streets paved at all. The only gold you're going to find is in the fillings in the cook's teeth over at the Texas Hot Lunch.

The streets have names, too, although you never hear anything about that. There isn't anything special about the names. They're just names like Main Street, Water Street, Grove Street, Vespar Street, and Church Street. Church Street was named after one of its first residents, Jerry Church. I know, you thought it was named for the churches. Nope, it was Jerry Church.

I can never understand why everyone is so concerned about the streets anyway. Where you have streets, you have cars, and cars are far more interesting—especially when they are convertibles. Yes sir, you can raise some real hell in a convertible.

Oh, I know, everyone in heaven is supposed to be an angel. Well, I can tell you that you are not going to find many angels, not under 18 anyway, and certainly not behind the wheel of repainted, souped-up, gas-guzzling convertibles cruising down Main Street with their radios blaring on a Saturday night. You may want to call them a lot of things, but I doubt that you would want to call the drivers angels.

Don't get me wrong. There are angels all right, but they become homecoming queens. You can see them over at the J. Arlington Painter Stadium, too, where the football team plays every Friday night in the fall. They're the ones in cheerleading outfits. By the way, those outfits are not all white, no matter what you've heard; they're purple and white with "BOBCATS" emblazoned across the front. What's the matter, didn't you think there were any bobcats in heaven? Well, any team that beats the Bellefonte Red Raiders and the Williamsport Millionaires in the same season deserves to go to heaven.

There are lawyers in heaven, too. It's the county seat, and there is always a courthouse in a county seat. And, of course, where there is a courthouse, there are lawyers. The situation is no different in heaven. I don't know why that should be so surprising!

There are doctors there, too. People get sick just like everywhere else. Only there, the doctors will make house calls if you are too sick to go to their office. Now you know you are in heaven!

You know it, too, because the whistle blows every day at five o'clock over at the paper mill; the elementary schools are named after Presidents like Lincoln and Roosevelt; everyone in town goes to the football games on Friday nights; the first day of trout season is a school holiday; girls have Ann as a middle name, like Jean Ann or Helen Ann or Emilie Ann; every boy who wants to become 13 has to walk out on a ledge called Peter's Steps; girls are smarter than boys, even after they get married; boys never grow up, even after they get married; it only costs 50 cents to go to the movies at the Roxy, the Martin, or the Garden theaters; a large ice-cream cone has four scoops; the monument at the corner of Bellefonte and Main streets is a traffic hazard; everyone swims in rivers and creeks rather than in swimming pools; fall is more beautiful than anything on earth; you don't wear shoes in the summer when you are a child; your best childhood friend is a dog; you have the same teachers that your parents had; you met your spouse at a dance at the teen canteen; Woolrich is not a clothing manufacturer but a town nearby; moving away from home means buying a house next door or, at the very worse, down the street; Dr. Louis S. Winner is called Butch and has been since first grade; and everyone knows everyone else.

Most people spend a lifetime worrying about whether or not they will get to heaven. They're not sure they know the way. Well, it really isn't hard to find: Just drive to Pennsylvania, get on Interstate 80, and get off at the Lock Haven exit. How do I know? Because I grew up there.

Teen Angel
May 1994

Teen Angel

How a young man found religion—with a
little help from the prettiest girl in church.

I consider myself a reasonably religious person, but I really can't tell you why. In fact, I really don't know what a religious person is. I just think that I am one.

Maybe it has something to do with my childhood. A good part of it was spent (many Sunday mornings, anyway) in Trinity Methodist Church. The church still stands on Main Street in Lock Haven, Pa. It is an enormous brick building with a large bell tower that received a coat of white paint about 40 years ago, and sometime later, a coat of yellow.

All the paint is gone now—and so are the Methodists. After serving a lifetime stewardship, they moved on to higher places. Most of their children, like me, moved away. And their church now stands empty.

It wasn't always that way. You could easily fit a thousand parishioners into that sanctuary, and on Easter Sundays they often did. On most other Sundays, though, there were lots of empty seats. Mine, however, was not one of them. No, sir. I came every Sunday until I graduated from high school.

It's not hard to remember why.

Some people were moved to come by the minister. Others were moved to come by the choir. I, however, was moved by an angel. Her name was Judy Haag (rhymes with vague).

Judy was the best-looking girl my age in the whole church. And she always sat alone down in front. Now, that was a serious problem because I always came to church late, and if I walked all the way down the aisle to the front and sat down beside her, everyone would see what I'd done. They would see that I had walked all the way down the aisle just to sit beside Judy Haag because she was the best-look-ing girl my age in church.

Knowing that I was being watched was certainly enough to cause me to pause before making the trip. But I always told myself that there was just as much reason for everyone to believe that I walked all the way down the aisle to the front of the church so I could hear the sermon better. That position, together with Judy Haag's, was always enough to help me justify the trip.

Of course, if I were going to be completely honest, I would have to tell you that Judy Haag's position carried more weight than how well I could hear the sermon. Nevertheless, whenever you are going to do something that is completely unjustified, it is important to try to justify it before you do it. And I always did before I walked down the aisle to sit in the front of the church near Judy Haag.

Actually, sitting down beside her was a lot tougher. It was not so easy to explain why the acoustics were better in that particular spot than anywhere else in the church. So I never did. The best spot, by the way, changed every Sunday morning and, amazingly, Judy always found it. All I had to do was find Judy. How do you explain something like that to the rest of the people in church? They would never understand, so I didn't even try.

I just tried to squeeze by Judy with a minimum of disturbance. She always looked up, said "Hi," and then smiled. What would you expect from an angel? Judy Haag never did anything wrong—except maybe grow too much.

She was really tall and I wasn't, and everyone could see that when we stood up during the hymns. I hated hymns because you had to stand to sing them, which was a stupid custom that should have been eliminated during the Reformation. I mean, if you are going to reform things, you should certainly include a barbaric custom like that, which can subject a 15-year-old boy to that kind of humiliation.

Since they didn't change the custom, I had to take matters into my own hands—or should I say toes? I stood on them every time we rose to sing a hymn. Now, if you have never tried to stand on your toes during four full stanzas of "Rock of Ages," you might be surprised to learn that the "Ages" are not the only things rocking by the time you are finished. Yes sir, it is pretty hard to keep your balance when the only thing between you and devastation is a set of 10 overworked toes.

To make matters worse, once a month the pastor passed out those pledge cards where you had to swear, with eternity at stake, that you never touched a drop of the hard stuff. How can you swear something like that, with those kinds of consequences, after teetering through four long stanzas of a hymn?

What a choice! I either had to look like a drunk or a dwarf. Considering all the consequences—including how things might look to Judy Haag—I chose to look like a drunk.

I never chose, however, to have my mother sing that loud. My mother sang in the choir, which was located in a loft above the pulpit directly in the front of the church. When she sang solos you could hear her over in the next county.

There is nothing more humiliating than having your mother make a public spectacle of herself, especially when you are sitting beside Judy Haag and everyone knows why. The only thing that I could ever think of doing on those occasions was slumping down in my seat so that no one could see me. Since they could anyway, and since they could now see that I was shorter than Judy Haag even when we were seated, deciding what to do was a difficult choice.

Now that I think about it, I guess that that's what I learned back at old Trinity Methodist Church: Religion involves a lot of difficult choices, some real risk, a little humility, and some very hard work. I guess I also learned over the years that it involves something more than Judy Haag.

Learning to Drive
June 1994

Learning to Drive

The principles of automobile science vs. common sense.

My mother, who lost both parents when she was a little girl, was raised by her Uncle John and Aunt Hannah Grove, as their only child, in a Pennsylvania German farming village called Lemont.

John and Hannah Grove were not much different from any other Pennsylvania German family. John grew up on a farm in a family of boys. The boys, including John, went to school for a good part of the day, did their chores when they got home, and spent much of the evening doing their homework. Whatever time was left was devoted to, in words commonly used by Pennsylvania Germans, "no good," which means, in our parlance, "raising a little hell."

On Saturdays, the boys helped out on the farm until "suppertime," which served as the transition between "God's work," which, of course, had already ended, and the "Devil's work," which was about to begin over at the dance at Hecla Park. On Sundays, they arose for a hearty breakfast followed by a morning filled with prayer, hymns, and scripture (by which they could seek redemption for the night before) and then a quiet afternoon at home.

Pennsylvania Germans believe, with some justification, that any time a Pennsylvania German boy is quiet on a Sunday afternoon he is "up to no good." Indeed, the Pennsylvania Germans believe, again with some justification, that the only chance a Pennsylvania German boy has in this life, given his errant nature, is to marry a Pennsylvania German girl. Not unmindful of this, John Grove married Hannah Behrer from over in Buffalo Run Valley.

It was not such a surprising choice. Hannah was neat "as a new pin," could sew "with the best of 'em," could "cook up a storm," and, "to top it all," was "pretty as a picture," as Pennsylvania Germans like to say. Most important, however, there was "no nonsense" about her.

Of course, there was really no nonsense about any Pennsylvania German girl. They understood that they were put on this earth to make something out of a Pennsylvania German boy. And, given the nature of Pennsylvania German boys, that was a pretty formidable task.

Hannah Grove was up to the task. With years of hard work and unbelievable patience—not to mention a little divine intervention—she turned that Pennsylvania German farm boy into a very successful farmer. But try as she did and "scold as she would," she could not get rid of the "tomfoolery." So when John Grove told her one Sunday afternoon in June that he was going to teach my mother, who was only 12 at the time, to drive, Hannah was livid. She was not about to allow him to risk "life and limb," especially the life and limb of her only niece, and she told him so.

John Grove was unmoved. Not that he did not ordinarily listen to his wife. The price of not doing so was too high. But where spiritual, metaphysical, or theological matters were involved—that is to say pride— it was quite another matter. And pride was involved here. Every boy in town could drive by the age of 14.

Hannah—who was far less spiritual, metaphysical, and theological than her husband, but, like the rest of her gender, a good deal more reasonable—reminded her husband that my mother was only 12, and a girl, too, and that everyone knew that girls were far less interested in cars, especially at 12.

This insight was not lost on John Grove, and he told his wife so, but he also reminded her in the same breath that my mother was a Grove. Hannah interrupted her husband at that point and advised him "in no uncertain terms" that not only was her niece a Grove but she was going to continue to be a Grove for the next 50 years, and that is why she was not going to drive at 12. Moreover, Hannah added "for good measure," my mother was only 12 and you can't teach a 12-year-old to drive. Why, she said, my mother probably couldn't even reach the pedals. Undaunted, John countered with a boast that, as a matter of fact, he could teach my mother to drive in an afternoon—that very afternoon. Absolutely disgusted, Hannah ended the conversation by saying, "There will be none of that!"

Now, if you are not Pennsylvania German, you may not understand the significance of such a directive when issued by a disgusted Pennsylvania German woman. In central Pennsylvania, where Pennsylvania Germans are found most frequently, it is said that such a directive, when issued by a Pennsylvania German woman, is the single biggest factor in the improvement of mankind—or, at the very least, the improvement of men in central Pennsylvania.

But John Grove was not interested in improvement on that Sunday afternoon in June, he was interested in teaching my mother to drive. So when his wife disappeared into the kitchen (John Grove may have been full of pride, but not stupidity), he immediately went over to the Beavers, where my mother was playing with her best friend, Ethel, and asked his niece if she wanted to go home and learn to drive. My mother was more than ready. So, together, they returned home and walked up to the barn behind the house, where John kept his Model A Ford.

There, John Grove spent the next 10 minutes explaining the principles of automobile science to my mother. When the lesson was over, he instructed her to jump up and sit in the driver's seat. After she was seated, he told her to "start the engine and put 'er in first." My mother started the engine and put 'er through the side of the barn. Startled by the racket, Hannah appeared at the back door. When John saw her, he hesitated a moment and then said, "It only took 15 minutes."

Hannah Grove (second from left) *and her niece, a Model A student, who is sitting on the fender of John Grove's car*

My 40th High School Reunion
October 1994

My 40th High School Reunion

Something I forgot to do keeps me going back home.

I don't know why high-school reunions are so significant, but I haven't missed one of mine in 40 years. And I won't miss the one next week, either. It has something to do with my childhood, I guess. There must be something back there that I forgot to do, but I really can't tell you what.

Oh, sure, I always wanted a chance to tell my teachers that they were wrong and my mother was right: I did amount to something after all. Maybe it's not what my mother thought it would be, but that's only because Bill Clinton got that job.

Now that I think about it, I suppose my successes wouldn't have impressed my teachers. They are all dead now, so they never would have known. Isn't that just like your old high-school teachers? They always get the last word.

I would also like to tell Allen Joslyn that I should have received the award for being the best-dressed boy in the class, not him. In nursery school, he looked like a mess. And he didn't improve much in the first grade, either. Things got better by third grade, but that's only because his girlfriend helped pick out his clothes. And she really wasn't that good at it. In fact, he's lucky that she broke up with him in 12th grade or he never would have had a chance. Somewhere in between he developed taste, but not anything like mine.

Funny, everyone said that's the reason why they decided to give him the award.

Here the author is seated between Helen Ann Shaffer (left), who wouldn't date him, and Judy Haag, who wouldn't marry him. Lou Lantz, whom Judy did marry, is right behind her. Chubby Shiavo, who rivaled the author in gridiron prowess, stands between Lou and Allen Joslyn, still a smarter dresser than the author. Wally Smith, still trim enough to play left field, stands next to Allen.

Country Living - October 1994

I would also like to ask Judy Haag (rhymes with vague) why she married Lou Lantz instead of me. When you think about it, the whole thing really doesn't make much sense. I was the only guy in the whole class who was shorter than she was, and you would think that a girl would notice something like that—especially a girl like Judy, who could have picked any guy she wanted. Instead, she chose some guy that was tall, nice looking, and rather well liked. Gee, that was half the guys in the class. Lou's only distinguishing characteristic was his intelligence. He was probably smarter than anyone else. Can you figure that out? I would never marry someone who was smarter than I was. Boy, there is just no accounting for girls. They do the dumbest things sometimes.

I would also like to talk to Chubby Schiavo about the time he made a game-saving tackle on me in a six-man football game between Penn and Roosevelt elementary schools. I had broken free on a beautiful open-field run and Chubby was the only thing between me and destiny. Well, destiny had to wait a while, because Chubby tackled me just before I crossed the goal line. When you think about it, that was a really selfish thing to do. In fact, that tackle alone probably cost him whatever chance he ever had, which was not much, of getting into Heaven. The tackle probably also cost me whatever chance I had of dating Helen Ann Shaffer in 12th grade. Girls don't ever forget things like that. Thankfully, we guys do.

Lastly, I would like to talk to Wally Smith about the tryouts for Little League baseball. He was chosen by the Elks and I wasn't. I just can't understand that. Wally was a pretty good left fielder, but I was much better. I certainly was a lot faster than he was on the base paths. And I could hit and field better than he could, too. I just couldn't do it in public.

But none of these things is what really keeps me going back home to my high-school reunions. Nope, the real reason I go back is something more. It's something that I almost forgot. It's simply to say thanks, thanks for memories.

Thanksgiving, Bah, Humbug!
November 1994

Thanksgiving, Bah, Humbug!

It's a good thing the Pilgrims didn't land in central Pennsylvania.

I don't remember exactly when it was that I first heard the story about the Pilgrims, but it must have been sometime in elementary school. I remember seeing pictures hanging on the classroom bulletin board that showed American Indians, Pilgrims, and their kids seated around the dinner table and celebrating Thanksgiving. And I remember thinking that if the Pilgrims had landed in central Pennsylvania instead of at Plymouth Rock, their kids would not have felt nearly so thankful.

You see, parents in central Pennsylvania were not anything like the Pilgrims. The Pilgrims, for starters, were always smiling. If you don't believe me, just take a close look at pictures of them. I'll bet you won't find a single Pilgrim without a smile, no matter what their kids were like.

That wasn't the case in central Pennsylvania when I was growing up, though.

You wouldn't find any smiling parents there, no matter what their kids were like.

And kids in central Pennsylvania were nearly perfect. I ought to know since I grew up there.

The Pilgrims were kinder to their kids, too. The Pilgrims only worried, for example, about whether their kids had enough to eat. In central Pennsylvania, parents worried that you had too much to eat. They were always saying, "If you eat one more piece of pumpkin pie, you're going to get sick to your stomach." Did you ever hear of a Pilgrim kid getting sick to his stomach from pumpkin pie?

I bet you never saw a picture of a Pilgrim kid taking care of the garden,

Country Living - November 1994

either. Nope, all they did was eat the stuff that grew in them. In central Pennsylvania, parents were the ones who did all the eating, and it was us kids who had to weed and water the garden. I don't know where we got our concept of justice in America, but I can tell you this—it didn't come from central Pennsylvania.

Schools did, though. Ever wonder why the Pilgrim kids looked so happy? They didn't have to go to school. Now there would be a reason for giving thanks! Oh, sure, everyone always tells you that you will appreciate your education later in life when you finally realize you could not have done without it. Well, the Pilgrim kids did alright without school. In fact, their descendants are really proud of them. You always hear people say proudly that they are the descendants of those who arrived on the Mayflower. Maybe if their ancestors had had to go to elementary school like I did they wouldn't be quite so proud of them. I mean, how often do you hear someone boast that his ancestor graduated from Roosevelt Elementary School?

You do hear, though, that the Pilgrims came to America to find religious tolerance. Well, I can tell you that they would not have found it in central Pennsylvania, not by a long shot. Try telling parents there that you don't want to go to Sunday school and see how long that's tolerated.

It would be tolerated just about as long as they would tolerate dinner guests that you had invited without getting their permission first. Yeah, the open-door policy ended with the Pilgrims as far as I was concerned. Every time I brought some of my friends home for dinner without asking my parents' permission first, they got angry. And when I let them know that their conduct was contrary to the great American open-door policy that began with the Pilgrims, they got even more angry. Obviously, we are talking guilty conscience here.

And imagine trying to get your parents' permission to dress the way the Pilgrims did. Sure, even I thought the Pilgrims looked a little funny; then again, when you're in elementary school, you tend to overlook stuff like that. You know that what people are really like has nothing to do with the way they look.

Not your parents, though. If your hair wasn't combed before you left for school in the morning, your mother would make you comb it, even though your hair was just going to get messed up at recess. If your jeans got dirty by the time you came home, she would make you wear a different pair the next day even though they were just going to get dirty, too. And, if you didn't dress up for Sunday school, your parents would have a fit even though you won't find anything about being dressed up in the Ten Commandments.

You won't find anything about how you're supposed to dress in the Mayflower Compact, either, and that's what the Pilgrims used to govern themselves. No, the Pilgrims knew that there were more important things in life. So they didn't care one bit about how anyone dressed for that very first Thanksgiving.

Well, you just see what happens if you don't dress up for Thanksgiving in central Pennsylvania. Unfortunately, parents there have lost the whole meaning of Thanksgiving.

Given that fact, someone asked me not long ago why I even bothered to celebrate Thanksgiving when I was young. Gosh, that's easy to answer-because the food was great!

The Godfather
January 1995

The Godfather

A story of friends and faux pas.

Lou Beres is one of my oldest friends. He was my roommate I during my freshman year of college. And he is my elder son Court's godfather.

Court has asked me many times why I chose Lou to be his godfather, since, according to the stories he's heard over the years, "some of the things that Lou did were unbelievable."

"Yes, they were," I've always answered. Then, repeating the stories, I've reminded Court that Lou attended college on a scholarship. And, while there, he became the president of the student body. On top of that, he was an excellent student.

"Yeah," Court said, "I remember all that, but what about the stories that involve you?"

"Well," I said, "Lou helped me to get a job at the sorority where he worked. He also took me home with him on holidays because I couldn't afford to travel all the way back from Chicago to central Pennsylvania. And, since I had never been away from home before, he showed me how to get around town.

"Yes," I continued, "Lou was a great friend; we never had a disagreement—except, possibly, for the time that I sat on his pillow. He had a thing about his pillow; but, when you think about how helpful he was. that was really a small thing."

"Well," said Court, "I don't think your first formal dance was such a small thing; that story is a lot different!"

"No, not really," I answered. "Not when you know the whole story."

You see, a girl named Lucy Jeffries had invited me to go to a formal dance. I had never been to a formal dance before. In fact, I didn't even know exactly what made one formal. I did know, however, that the dance was going to take place at a sorority—although I wasn't quite sure what sororities were. I just knew that they had good-looking girls in them, which meant that an invitation by one of them to attend a formal dance was extraordinarily significant. And I treated it accordingly: I asked Lou what to do.

He told me that I had to rent a tuxedo. When I asked him what that would cost, he said that it would probably cost more than a white

Country Living - January 1995   107

dinner jacket. So I decided that it would be better to rent a white dinner jacket instead.

The owner of the rental agency disagreed. He kept repeating that white dinner jackets were worn only during the summer and that this was winter. Lou, who could see through any scam, asked if that was because white dinner jackets were not warm enough to be worn in the winter. The owner, visibly taken aback, replied that we were missing the point.

Lou, who clearly saw the point, then asked the owner if it would cost less to rent a white dinner jacket than a tuxedo in the winter. The owner now looked at us like we had lost our minds and said that he had never thought about that because no one had ever rented one in the winter. "Then they should cost less to rent," Lou said, "and maybe that's why you don't want to rent one to us."

The owner became angry and, for reasons I cannot explain, changed his mind and decided to rent the dinner jacket to us after all—and at a fraction of what a tuxedo would have cost. He said, still angry, that I deserved it—obviously referring to the huge discount.

The owner then handed me a large box that contained a dinner jacket and everything that goes with it, and asked, "Are you Greek?"

"No," I answered, "I'm Pennsylvania German."

Trying to hide the smile that had inexplicably appeared on his face, he said, "I mean are you in a fraternity—you know—the ones with the Greek letters?"

"Oh. No," I replied. Then, remembering that the only people you could really trust, aside from your freshman roommate, were the ones back home in central Pennsylvania, I asked indignantly, "How do I know that the dinner jacket will fit me?"

"Trust me," he answered, almost before I had finished the question, "it will fit you perfectly, especially in the winter."

I'm not sure Lou heard him,

though, because the smile that had inexplicably developed on his face, too, had now broken into outright laughter.

It was not a laughing matter, however, when I opened the box on the night of the dance and tried to put on the shirt I'd rented. All of the buttons were off. When I told Lou, he just smiled (apparently because he didn't want me to get any more upset than I was) and said not to worry because he would sew some on. Boy, did I feel stupid; I couldn't even sew.

On the other hand, I could put on a tie; but I was not about to put on the one I found in the box. It was a bow tie like the ones farmers wore to church on Sundays in central Pennsylvania. So I put on a regular tie—you know, the kind that hangs down to your waist—and showed it to Lou. He thought it was too conservative and gave me one of his own. It was pink and black.

I put it on and looked in the mirror. Boy, did it look great; pink and black was really big that year. I turned around to show Lou, with a look of relief on my face, and said, "I just didn't want to look like an ol' farmer."

Lou smiled and assured me that "No farmer ever looked like that!" I guess even Lou thought that I was quite a sight.

The sight of the black patent-leather shoes in the box was another thing entirely. College guys didn't wear patent-leather shoes. In fact, nobody wore them except little girls who carried their pennies in a purse to match.

Well, I was not about to wear shoes like that. What I was about to wear were my white bucks—until Lou intervened. He said that mine had dirt on them and his did not, so I ought to wear his, instead. That was just like Lou. He was always worried about what I was doing. And he would always say that it was important not to create the wrong kind of impression. But I don't think there was any doubt in Lou's mind about what kind of impression I would make here.

There was no doubt, either, about my impression of the last thing in the box.

Lou called it a cummerbund and told me that you wear them around your waist.

Now, I wasn't born yesterday; guys wear belts around their waist. No, this was obviously meant to be worn a little higher up—around your chest. So that's where I put it. Then, feeling rather proud, I walked over to Lou so that he could see what I looked like with everything on. He was speechless. Well, what can you say when you see perfection!

I'll tell you what Lucy Jeffries said. She said that such attire might be my idea of funny, but it wasn't hers. She told me to put the cummerbund down where it belonged and to go back home and put on a bow tie and black shoes. So I did.

Court, who had never heard this part of the story before, said, "I bet the rest of the evening was a mess."

"No," I replied, "it actually went rather well." In fact, I thought that Lucy had sort of forgotten about the whole thing until she asked me if I would like to go with her to a costume party the next week. And then she added, with a little smile on her face, "I don't imagine that you will have any difficulty thinking of something to wear."

"No," I replied, without any smile on my face, "I'll get Lou to help; he has such a great sense of humor."

Court, who had now heard enough, frowned and said, "I don't think he had such a great sense of humor."

"Actually," I explained, "he did."

"Why?" asked Court impatiently. "Because he laughed when he got back to the room and discovered what had happened to you?"

"No," I said. "Because he laughed when he got back to the room and discovered that I had used his pillow to clean the floor."

Being Different
March 1995

Being Different

Most kids strive to be like everybody else.
My buddy Allen had different ideas.

We all have burdens to bear when we are growing up, and mine was called Allen Joslyn. Allen was one of my best friends, but that was not the problem. No, the problem was that he was different.

Allen was very smart, and it is not so good to be so smart when you are growing up. At least it isn't good to appear to be so smart. Allen wasn't smart enough to know that, but I was. Yes, I was always trying to explain to everyone that Allen was just one of the guys, even though no guy ever talked like he did. Allen was incapable of using words that you didn't need a dictionary to understand. Well, I couldn't understand them, anyway.

I couldn't understand why Allen always had to have paint all over his clothes, either. Oh, sure, he was a tremendous artist, but he didn't have to advertise that fact. I mean, who ever chooses an artist to be on his football team? No one, that's who.

Oh, all right, I did sometimes, but only after explaining to everyone else on the team that the only reason Allen looked the way he did was because his family couldn't afford to buy him any other clothes. Of course, it didn't help matters that he came from a prominent family that owned one of the largest houses in town.

But that wasn't the only dumb thing Allen did. He did dumb things quite frequently. I remember, for instance, the time that he decided to build some mountains on the electric train board that my parents always put up on top of the coffee table in the living room every year at Christmas. A little village was over on one side, and Allen said the board lacked symmetry. So he decided to solve the problem by building mountains on the other side.

I knew that building mountains on that board was not going to solve

*Allen and Cal playing chess—
Cal refuses to say who won.*

any problems. In fact, I knew that it was going to cause problems. I knew it because it was Allen's idea, and because I was a student of history. All of Allen's ideas had caused a mess in the past.

This time would be no different. I knew that as soon as I saw Allen haul ashes up from my basement to the living room and dump them on top of the train board. My parents did not ordinarily put ashes in the living room. Certainly, they had never dumped two feet of them on top of the electric train board. But Allen said that he needed that amount to make mountains that would look like the Swiss Alps. Frankly, I could not imagine how he would make that pile of ashes look like the Swiss Alps. I couldn't even imagine how he would make them look like mountains; but I certainly could imagine how he would make the board look a big mess.

To be honest with you, though, I never imagined that Allen would use plaster of paris to do it. He poured the stuff all over the ashes, then he molded everything to look like the Alps and painted it accordingly. When he finished, he said, "Now you can't tell the difference."

What I could tell, when the plaster of paris started drying, was that the whole mess was beginning to look permanent, and I knew, without being told, that my parents would not like to have that mess permanently in their living room. Allen said that I was always worrying prematurely and that my parents would probably not object to leaving the board up all year-round when they saw what he had done to it. Well, he was right about one thing: It was premature to worry about taking the electric train board down after Christmas, especially when the legs of the coffee table collapsed.

My parents cleaned up the mess when they came home several hours later. To their credit, they didn't get nearly as upset as they did the time that Allen and I got lost in a canoe on our way up Bald Eagle Creek to the town of Beech Creek. Naturally, it was Allen's idea. He said that even though the 30-mile stretch was virtually impassable, we could do it in a canoe, which rides high enough to make it through the rapids and which is light enough to carry around the shallows. What's more, Allen said, he would rig up a motor to the canoe so we would not have to paddle the whole way and we could make it back home before dark.

Now, I knew immediately that this was a crazy idea. I knew it because it was Allen's and because everyone always said that you couldn't make it up the Bald Eagle to Beech Creek, let alone in a day. Nevertheless, against my better judgment, I agreed to try. After all, if we made it, we would be the talk of the town, including the part that Phyllis Karstetter lived in and I had been crazy about her for years.

Well, we became the talk of the town all right, but not because we made it to Beech Creek. We didn't make it to Beech Creek. We didn't make it because the stupid motor that Allen had rigged up to the back of the canoe broke down part of the way there. Just great. He couldn't do anything right.

Then, of course, we lost an hour while he tried to fix it. Naturally, he couldn't. So we tried to paddle the rest of the way. Have you ever tried to paddle a canoe upstream for 20 miles, not to mention carry it for another five? When you are 12, it's exhausting.

After hours and hours, I noticed that the sun was going down. Allen said that there was no reason to worry because it was only 12 noon according to his watch and we were nearly there. Yeah, sure. Who knew where we were. And all of a sudden the sun decided to go down at 12 noon?

Allen said that the sun always sets earlier this far north, but it stays daylight up here forever, and, moreover, his watch was guaranteed by the maker to lose no more than a minute a week. Well, when the maker made that guarantee, it had in mind the normal user. The maker did not have in mind some idiot who would stick his hand in the water, with the watch on it, while he tried to fix a stupid motor. Yes, if the maker had decent legal counsel, it would have made an exception to this guarantee for idiots. Since it did not, the maker, the legal counsel, and I were in serious trouble.

How did I know? Because a search party that had reached us shortly before dark told us that our parents had been desperately looking for us for hours. And, as if that were not enough, they told us that the whole town had been enlisted in the search. The local radio station had been issuing hourly bulletins. Piper Cubs were searching the area by air. The state police had joined in the effort.

Great. There goes Phyllis Karstetter. For that matter, there goes whatever chance I had in life. I was certain to be the laughingstock of the whole seventh grade—maybe the whole junior high school. All because of him!

I knew then that someday I wanted to study law because of my new-found interest in the concept of "justifiable homicide." And one day I did—study law, that is. Allen? Well, he graduated in the top ten of his high-school class, graduated from Haverford College with honors, attended a graduate program at Oxford University in England, and graduated from Harvard Law School. Amazing, isn't it, how someone so dumb could be that smart?

Recess
June 1995

Recess

When the going got tough, the tough got rougher.

I remember being in fifth grade in Roosevelt Elementary School. I remember it all right, but I don't remember it very fondly.

I was always getting into trouble. And I never really knew why. I wasn't much different from all the other boys in the class. They were always in trouble, too.

We were always talking too much, except, of course, when the fifth-grade teacher asked us a question. Then we didn't talk at all. Not because we didn't know the answer, but because we were exceedingly modest.

We were also brilliant engineers, which you could tell from the design of the paper airplanes that we sailed around the classroom periodically. We were way ahead of our time in fashion, too. We introduced the relaxed, casual look before the fashion industry even knew what it was. Nothing but blue jeans, with holes in them, mind you, old sweatshirts, and dirty tennis shoes for us. And we always remembered not to comb our hair.

We also remembered to do all of the things that were most important in life first. This was made clear by when we turned in our homework papers—late.

Fifth-grade girls didn't seem to have any of these qualities, though. No, they had no sense of priority and, consequently, always turned in their homework papers on time. They were also light-years behind in fashion. Every day, they wore clothes that matched, and clean ones at that. Why, they wouldn't have known casual if it had hit them over the head. I mean, you never saw a fifth-grade girl with her hair messed up. They didn't know how!

They couldn't design paper airplanes that would sail around the room, either. And modesty was simply not part of their vocabulary—at least not the vocabulary that they used to answer every question that the teacher asked, all day long.

But, despite these shortcomings, girls did better than boys in fifth grade—a lot better. And they never got in trouble. Yeah, it was enough to make you sick. Well, it certainly made us sick—of girls anyway. I guess that's why we never played with them at recess.

It was a good thing, too, because the game we played was far too rough for girls. In our game, called Every Man Come Across, the guys who were it stood in the middle of the field and tried to tackle the ones who were not it as soon as they left the goal line on one side of the field and began running toward the goal line on the opposite side.

There was never a day that we did not enjoy playing this game at recess. That is until the winter day when True Talley told her cousin Butch Winner that the only reason Roosevelt had lost the football game to Penn Elementary School the previous fall was because none of the guys on our team knew how to tackle. True also said that there was not a fifth-grade girl at Roosevelt who couldn't tackle better than that. Butch, who was better known for his football prowess than his judgment, angrily responded that if the girls thought that they could tackle better than the boys, maybe they would like to try at recess.

Unfortunately for us, they did.

And the first one they tackled was ole Butch. Now, Butch Winner was the toughest guy in fifth grade at Roosevelt.

Everyone in school knew it, including the girls. When ole Butch got up a head of steam. there wasn't anything created by the Almighty that could bring him down, not even big Chubby Schiavo over at Penn. So when ole Butch took off across that field, we knew that nothing could stop him—nothing human anyway.

And it wasn't! It wore a pink coat with mittens and leggings to match, a green muffler wrapped around its neck several times, and a green tasseled cap pulled way down over its head so that only its pigtails stuck out. With all that paraphernalia on, you might think it couldn't run very fast, but it did. Amazingly, it caught poor Butch just before he crossed the goal line. Darn near killed him with a flying tackle that would have made every professional football player in America proud. To this day, ole Butch walks sort of funny because of that tackle.

The guys in fifth grade said that

Ready for recess, the author's fifth-grade class, including him (seated, third from right), *Butch Winner* (standing, next to the teacher), *and their arch-nemeses True Talley and Judy Haag* (seated, fifth and sixth from left).

Butch was tackled by a creature from hell. The girls said that the only creature that wore an outfit like that was True Talley.

Wally Smith was another matter. He wasn't as tough as Butch, but he was really smart. Wally was so smart that he tied Barbara Dilling for the best average in the class a year earlier. And he never even studied. All the guys said that if Wally studied just half as much as Barbara did, he would have beaten her hands down. Yeah, you had to get up pretty early in the morning to get ahead of ole Wally.

That's why I can't explain what happened next: Wally, who was never the fastest guy in the world, moved, from bush to bush, right down the field. Barbara Dilling, though, was waiting behind a bush up ahead of him. When Wally reached that bush, she flattened him with one of the wickedest hits you have ever seen. Can you believe that? It had to be Barbara Dilling!

Well, the guys said that didn't prove anything. The girls said, "Oh yes it does!"

I don't know what Donny Witmyer proved. I guess he proved that fifth-grade girls were capable of liking a fifth-grade boy. Yep, they all liked ole Donny. So when Donny took off down the field, we guys felt pretty certain that no girl was going to try to kill him. At least not until Marietta Webb did.

It was merciless. Marietta, who was bigger than poor Donny, buried him in one of the most vengeful tackles you have ever seen.

We couldn't explain it. The girls could, though. They said that Donny was a jerk because he snickered when Marietta had sung her camp song, "Down on the Banks of the Hanky Panky," at show-and-tell a week earlier, when he knew (or should have known) that she really liked him, and so he got what he deserved. The guys, who were really taken aback by the ominous implications of all of this, decided that whoever said that hell has no fury like a woman scorned was right.

Well, we were furious, too. The girls had absolutely destroyed our best hopes. And now everything was riding on me. Not that that was all bad. It's true, I was the smallest guy in the class, but I was also the fastest. No guy had beaten me in a race since first grade. In fact, I had never lost a race until Judy Haag beat me the fall they let girls run, too. The guys said that race wasn't fair because Judy was wearing a dress and you can run faster in a dress. "Oh, yeah?" the girls responded. "Well, tell him to put on a dress and then let's see who's faster." Because some things are easier said than done, I didn't take up their challenge at the time.

I did now, though. With the guys' cheers echoing in my ears, I took off like a blazing comet right down that field. Yeah, I thought, let's see if Judy Haag can catch me when she's got leggings on. Well, we didn't have to wait long to see. She caught me about a quarter of the way down the field. Looking around, I realized that not one guy was left standing. "Can you believe it?" I said. "Someday, some poor guy is going to marry those girls."

Peter's Steps
July 1995

Peter's Steps

Boys walk a fine line on their
way to becoming men.

My hometown is In the Allegheny Mountains of central Pennsylvania. It rests alongside the West Branch of the Susquehanna River, which cut a beautiful valley into the Appalachian Mountains on its way southeastward toward Harrisburg and, eventually, to Chesapeake Bay. The beauty of the valley, which is called the Bald Eagle Valley after a Susquehannock Indian Chief, drew some of the early pioneers who had been traveling westward toward Pittsburgh. Two of the better known were Jerry Church and Peter Grove: Jerry Church because he founded the town and Peter Grove because he fell off a ledge over on the other side of the river. In his honor, the townspeople named the ledge Peter's Steps.

Oh, sure, everyone says that he really didn't fall; they say he leaped into the river below in order to escape some of Chief Bald Eagle's men. It seems that the Chief was disgusted with all the tobacco that Peter Grove had planted down below the town where the Susquehanna divides briefly to form a great island, which the townspeople aptly call Great Island. It seems the Chief just loved Great Island, and that it was rapidly becoming polluted with tobacco smoke. If there was one thing the Chief could not stand, it was air pollution.

So he, or rather some of his men, confronted Peter Grove about the problem up on that ledge. Of course, Peter Grove, being a Pennsylvania German, did not deal very well with confrontation or, for that matter, any other kind of emotion, and to avoid the confrontation, or any other kind of emotion, he, according to the story, leaped into the river below.

Now, when you are a young boy in my town, listening to older boys tell you that Peter Grove had walked out on that ledge, that they had walked out on that ledge, and that everyone in town who is a man had walked out on that ledge is not very comforting. Like every boy in town, I had some interest in becoming a man.

For that reason, I decided that I had better walk out there, too. I also decided that I had better not discuss that fact with my mother. There are certain things that a 12-year-old boy should not discuss with his mother, and one of them is that he is about to do something stupid that is going to result in his death. A guy just can't expect his mother to understand a thing like that!

If she could, she would realize that the kind of death that would result from walking out on that ledge would be far quicker than the one that would result from not doing it. That death would last as long as the memory of every other 12-year-old boy in town.

Realizing this fact, I decided to make sure that every one of those boys believed that I had walked out on that ledge. I say believed because I had no intention of doing it. No, sir, my mother didn't raise me to be an idiot.

Of course, she didn't raise me to lie, either, but she never had to walk out on that ledge. If she had, she might have understood what Machiavelli meant when he said there are occasions when it is more noble to lie. Since I did—understand that fact and have to walk out on that ledge—knew that one of those occasions had arrived.

I also knew that I needed someone to go with me to confirm that I did what I didn't. Now, the kind of person you needed to do something like that was someone who could understand why you wanted him to do it. So that person would

have to be another 12-year-old boy who had to walk out on that stupid ledge, too.

That's why I chose Wally Smith. Oh, sure, I also chose Wally because he was smart. I mean, maybe he'd read Gulliver's Travels more often than he'd read Machiavelli, but Wally was smart enough to know that if he walked out on that ledge, the only place he would be traveling would be straight down. Wally also had a lot of character. Yes sir, you want someone you can depend on in circumstances like that.

Well, as it turned out, I couldn't—depend on him, I mean. When we got up there, Wally's judgment became clouded by his character. Although he had promised me he would, he just couldn't lie about the whole thing. Can you believe that? After all my planning, we get up there and he gets an attack of character.

In fact, that's not the half of it. He decided that he had to do the right thing, even if I didn't, and walk across that stupid ledge himself. Well, if he really wanted to do the right thing, he should have fallen off and spared me a lifetime of suffering. But no, he didn't fall off like any reasonable person; he made it the whole way across. Disgusting, isn't it?

Well, looking back, I learned a lot of things from this experience. The biggest, by far, was that you can't trust someone with a lot of character.

The Guy in the Mirror
October 1995

The Guy in the Mirror

He reminded me of somebody, but who?

My younger son, Lars, graduated from the Mercersburg Academy in Mercersburg, Pa. So did the famous Hollywood actor Jimmy Stewart about 50 years earlier. In between a lot of other people did, too. But the students I remember most are Jake Keliikipi, Michael McMahon, and David Confair—Lars's roommates.

They were all Pennsylvania boys. Maybe that's why I remember them so well. But, then, maybe not; maybe there was something more. Jake was from the town of Washington, Pa., over near Pittsburgh. Mike was from Easton, not too far from Philadelphia, on the other side of the state. Dave was from Williamsport, which is in central Pennsylvania, just about 20 miles from my hometown, Lock Haven. I guess I remember ole (which is what we in central Pennsylvania call someone that we like a lot) Dave Confair the best of all, but I really can't tell you why.

Dave was easy to like, when you got to know him. He was reserved, very re-served, and if you grew up somewhere other than in central Pennsylvania you might say he was shy. But ole Dave Confair was not shy, not to a central Pennsylvania boy like me, anyway. No, sir. His was the kind of reserve that you always maintained around your parents, your schoolteachers, and other adults so that they would not be disappointed to learn that underneath the quiet façade was a lot more than they ever imagined.

Well, there was certainly a lot more to Dave Confair than anyone would have imagined on first meeting him. When you were around him for a little while, you began to see the wit. But not easily, mind you. It was not very direct, and it really was quite wry. I guess it is that way with those of us from central Pennsylvania. We are not very direct, so you have to listen carefully or you might miss our subtle kind of humor. Sort of like in my columns.

You certainly couldn't miss the eccentricities—Dave's, I mean. He used to clean his room at Mercersburg at least twice a week. How many 17-year-old fellows did you know who were that neat? Dave was that neat. Of course, he roomed with Lars at the time, who was not that neat, and that certainly explains

Country Living - October 1995 131

part of it, but not all. No, Dave was just plain neat even to someone like me who prides himself on being neat. Only I was never eccentric.

Dave was also very organized. Everyone knows that 17-year-old boys are not very organized, but Dave was. Yes, sir, at Mercersburg he used to reorganize his room at least once a week. Lars was lucky that he wound up in the same room when Dave got finished.

You have to admire that kind of orderliness. We always did in central Pennsylvania, anyway. They don't anywhere else, though. No, ever since I left home, everyone has always told me that I am compulsive.

Well, there was nothing compulsive about the way ole Dave would fish. He was a great trout fisherman—even by our standards in central Pennsylvania, where everyone was a good fisherman. Everyone there also liked to tell stories about their fish, and they were likely to exaggerate a little bit about how many they caught and how big they were.

Dave was not much different, but I was. I always made it a practice not to exaggerate, and I never really liked telling stories—especially ones about where I grew up and the people who lived there.

I did like to play tennis, though. So did ole Dave Confair. But Dave was a better tennis player than I ever was. He was a natural. Funny, for some people, when they are young, most things come rather easily. Dave Confair was one of those people. So was I once. Gosh, to think that I had almost forgotten.

I had also forgotten to go home—to central Pennsylvania-after I finished school. Not ole Dave Confair, though. No, he didn't forget where he came from or who he was. He went right back to what made him that way because being that way was kind of special even if it was different.

I never forgot how different Dave Confair was, but I did forget who he reminded

The author (left) and Dave Confair as students.

me of. It was someone who lived in central Pennsylvania a long time ago. He was a little eccentric like ole Dave and he was certainly as reserved, but with a wry sense of humor, too. And he liked to tell stories about where he grew up and the people who lived there—like ole Dave Confair. Unlike Dave Confair, however, he never went home.

A Town, a Trout, and a Tall Tale
November 1995

A Town, a Trout, and a Tall Tale

A country boy's magnificent obsession.

I grew up in a central Pennsylvania town called Lock Haven, which is only about 20 miles from another town called Bellefonte, which was founded in the 18th century. Between then and now, Bellefonte has produced seven state governors, who lived in beautiful old homes on streets now named after them.

The town has also produced a lot of beautiful girls with shapely legs—legs that got that way, according to

The author poses in front of Andrew Gregg Curtin, one of Bellefonte, Pa.'s seven state governors.

fellows in Lock Haven, because the girls they belonged to had to walk up and down Belletonte's hilly streets all the time. Bellefonte, like Rome, was built on seven hills. It was also built alongside the big spring from which it got its French name.

Most fellows growing up with me in Lock Haven were not interested in French, so we didn't much care about the name of the town. We didn't care about history, either, so the governors and their houses were not very interesting to us. The girls were, of course, but not as much as something else in Bellefonte. Yeah, there was something else we found far more appealing: the trout in the big spring.

Lock Haven boys like big fish and those trout were big fish. They got that way by living a long time. They were able to do that because no one was allowed to catch them; it was against the law. Now, law may have been important to those Bellefonte governors, but a little law never stood in the way of a Lock Haven boy like me—not where big fish were concerned, anyway. No, the problem was not legal; the program was logistical. Living in Lock Haven,

Country Living - November 1995

I was too far away to catch one of those big Bellefonte trout.

Realizing that fact, I got a summer job driving a laundry truck in Bellefonte. If you want to catch big fish, you have to go where they are. The trouble was that none of the fish ever had any shirts that needed to go to the cleaners. So I never had any reason to stop where they were. I did stop everywhere else in town, though, and that took all of my time. That's the trouble with a job—you have to spend all your time working.

Not that the work was uninteresting. The governors were interesting people, and, except for the one who was a statue in front of the courthouse, they were quite friendly. The governors were also antiques collectors, and collecting antiques was interesting, too. Of course, collecting antiques was a serious disease. It was highly contagious and once you got it there was no recovery. You were condemned to spend the rest of your life buying old things no one else wanted.

Well, after being around all those antiques, I became afflicted; I started spending all of my free time buying useless objects. Actually, I didn't spend all of my time doing that; I spent some of it looking at all those good-looking Bellefonte girls. Then, after a while and a little comparison shopping, I decided to spend my time with just one Bellefonte girl.

She was the only thing that I could think of to save myself from acquiring the whole 18th century. And she also provided me with the perfect cover. People who wanted to know what my intentions were would have been surprised that I was interested in doing something wrong, all right, but with something that could swim underwater longer than she could.

As it turned out, the only wrong thing I ever did around her was to use the English language. Compared to her, I didn't do it very well. I'm not talking just about conversation, either; I'm talking about writing, too. She was a great writer. I guess it was because she had such a big vocabulary. So did the rest of her family, for that matter. In fact, they used to play word games during dinner all the time and everyone in the family always did better at them than I did, even her baby sister. The only one I ever beat was the family dog—and he tied me twice.

After that, she felt so sorry for me that she used to drive me out on a lonely road behind the high school and park, where no one could see us, and teach me how to write. Unbelievable! I spent the whole evening parked with one of the best-looking girls in Bellefonte and all that happened was that my writing improved.

Things got worse. I started to spend more time writing about fish than catching them. That's when I knew that I had to get out of that relationship. I was beginning to lose all perspective. I mean, a few more months of parking with her and I might start writing articles for magazines!

To avoid such a fate, I decided to go to college at Penn State, which is located only about five miles away from Bellefonte, the big spring, and all those trout.

While there, I decided to major in philosophy. When you plan to walk five miles to Bellefonte in the dead of night so no one can see you illegally fish for trout that you will never catch because they are older and wiser than you are, it is important to develop a reason for doing so. What better way to do that than by spending four years in the department of philosophy? After all, isn't that where they study lunatics who spend a lifetime trying to justify an unreasonable obsession?

Well, even after four years of trying, I never could justify mine. So, I decided, upon graduation, to go to law school. If you can't philosophically justify doing something illegal, you'd better prepare to legally defend it. So I did, and after I graduated from law school three years later, I became so busy practicing law that I never had time to go back and try to catch one of those Bellefonte trout.

Incredible, isn't it? I left Lock Haven to catch one of those big fish and the only thing that happened after 40 years is that I went to college, became a writer, practiced law, and tried to collect most of the antiques in the United States. Yeah, after 40 years, I have nothing to show for it!

Growing Up
January 1996

Growing Up

It takes time, but it happens.

I was miserable when I was growing up. Oh, sure, my parents were okay. In fact, looking back now, they were great. So were my friends, and I had a lot of them. School was all right, too. But none of these things compensated for my size. Yes, I was so short that the best-looking girl in the whole universe, Helen Ann Shaffer, who just happened to be in my class, couldn't even see me.

Steve Romeo, who masqueraded as one of my best friends, always said that I was the one who couldn't see, because everyone knew that Helen Ann considered me to be one of her best friends. But I didn't want to be one of her best friends. Steve wondered why and I really wasn't sure, but I was sure that best friends always did things with each other and every time I did something with Helen Ann, I ended up looking like an idiot.

I remember, for instance, the time in seventh grade when Helen Ann wanted me to try out for the part of a dwarf called Rumpelstiltskin in a play by that name to be put on in the rose garden of the local library. Helen Ann had already gotten the part of the miller's beautiful daughter who was ordered by the king to spin straw into gold. Of course, the miller's daughter couldn't do it, so she entered into an arrangement with Rumpelstiltskin, who had agreed to do it for her on the condition that she give him her firstborn child. Well, when the king saw all of that gold, he married the miller's beautiful daughter and, sure enough, Rumpelstiltskin demanded their firstborn child.

The play didn't end there, but my life may as well have. That certainly would have been better than playing the part of a dwarf. Yeah, when you're short, the last thing in the world you need to do is be a dwarf—especially a mean one. Besides, when you're allergic to roses, the last place in the world you need to be is in the library rose garden. You end up being a mean little dwarf with a drippy nose. Just the thing to impress Helen Ann.

Steve said it must have left some impression because Helen Ann insisted that I take French with her in ninth grade. Boy, was that a mistake. Little people can't speak French. They can't pronounce the vowels right; they can't get their mouths around them. And their little minds can't remember all of the French words. Even worse, their little voices are high-pitched. How do you speak a Romance language like that with a high-pitched voice? It certainly isn't very romantic. About the only thing that you appeal to is a cricket—a French cricket.

Steve said that Helen Ann apparently liked the way I sounded when I played the piano because she encouraged me to play it at our junior high school commencement. Oh, sure, I remember that; it was the dumbest thing I ever did. There were more than a thousand people in the auditorium and the piano was up on the stage. That meant that I had to walk all the way down the aisle in order to play it. That's right! I had to walk all the way down there—all by myself—in front of all those people who knew that I was going to mess up.

That's hard enough to do when you're a big guy to start with, but it's even more difficult when you are not. For one thing, it takes longer to get there because you take smaller steps. And, for another, you grow smaller with each step you take. So, by the time that you get there you're little more than a dot. And everyone is wondering how a dot is going to play the piano.

Steve said that it reminded him of the time that Helen Ann convinced me to play mixed doubles with her in the tennis tournament put on by the town every year. Of course, I had been trying to forget that episode since the day it happened. Imagine, me playing mixed doubles with Helen Ann Shaffer. I must have been out of my mind. Not that I wasn't a pretty good tennis player.

All through high school, playing tennis with Steve and Helen Ann was about all I ever did during summer vacations. But playing mixed doubles in a tennis tournament was quite another thing.

Yeah, in mixed doubles, a good-looking girl always picks a guy to play with her who is big enough to hit those powerful first

"Little dreams my dainty dame, Rumpelstiltskin is my name"—the author spins straw into gold.

serves and those booming overhead slams. She also wants some big hulking guy who can dominate net play during her serves. Well, Helen Ann's hulk couldn't see over the net!

He couldn't jump over it, either. That's right! Twice I got my foot caught on the top of the net as I tried to jump over it and shake hands with the players on the other side. It was really embarrassing. Have you ever tried shake hands with someone while you are hanging upside down from a net?

Steve said that Helen Ann must not have been too embarrassed because in 11th grade she asked me to go with her to a big dance at Heckla Park. Gosh, I had almost forgotten. That sure was a fabulous time. The great Glen Miller Orchestra played and we danced all night. I didn't even notice that Helen Ann was taller. Now how do you explain that?

Steve said that I must have grown up. Funny, I don't think that I had gotten any taller.

Learning to Ride a Bicycle
March 1996

Learning to Ride a Bicycle

Lessons on a two-wheeler.

Learning to ride a bicycle is a very serious thing in a boy's life. It is a very serious thing because you can get very seriously hurt. But there is much more to it than that. You can learn a lot of serious lessons, too.

Among other things, you learn that your parents are frauds and that they really didn't mean it when they pretended to care about you for the first seven years of your life. Why else would they let go of your bike when it's moving?

Oh, sure, you had your suspicions during all that potty-training stuff. And then they abandoned you on the first day of school to that witch teaching kindergarten.

But they assured you, in unqualified terms, during the meeting in the principal's office, which was called because you bit the witch on the arm, that they still cared for you and that, notwithstanding this unfortunate incident, they would be with you for the rest of your life.

Well, where were they now? I'll tell you where they were. They were standing six feet behind you, without ever having told you that they had let go, shouting "Pedal, pedal, pedal!" instead of "Put your foot down!" which is what you tried to do just before the bike veered out of control and crashed into your dad's new car. And, to top it off, your dad was more concerned about the scratch on his automobile than the compound fracture of your knee.

Can you believe that? They just don't care about you anymore. Heck, they'll probably want you to go to college all by yourself, too.

But that's not all you discover. No, you discover that everyone likes little girls more than they like little boys. How do you discover that? By looking at the crossbar, that's how. You have one and they don't. Yeah, they can put their feet down on the ground and you can't. It is the single biggest factor in explaining why women live longer than men.

Of course, you don't have to ride a bike that has a crossbar. That's right. You don't have to crash all the time; you can put your feet down just like the girls do. Yeah, you can be the only guy in the whole universe who rides a girl's bike. And, while you're at it, you can do your homework on time and get good grades, too.

I know, when you look at it that way, it is a lot easier to ride a bicycle that has a crossbar. Yeah, when you're a guy it can be pretty hard if you're not smart enough to do all the dumb things that every other guy does.

You don't have to be very smart, how-ever, to tell the difference between Republican and Democratic parents when you're trying to learn how to ride a bicycle. Sure, the Democrats hold on to the bicycle longer; the Republicans let go right away. And they cheer louder if you don't crash. On the other hand, if you do crash, the Democrats will call an ambulance even if you're not hurt. The Republicans will tell you to ignore it and get back up and try again even if you just lost a leg.

Of course, some parents are not members of either party. Yeah, they're independents. And they're not hard to identify, either. They're the ones who say that the responsibility for learning to ride a bicycle ought to be given back to children. They say that adults have forgotten what children want and that children can learn by themselves.

When you're young, you learn not to take these parents too seriously. After all, you don't want to have to walk for the rest of your life.

Actually, if you think about it, you do—want to walk the rest of your life. For that reason, you may want to determine what kind of medical care is available before you get on a two-wheeler. You can never be too careful about medical care. Coverage for bicycle accidents may not be provided under your family's hospitalization insurance. In fact, many hospitalization policies specifically exclude self-inflicted injuries.

Of course, you can always argue that your parents made you do it. And if the insurance examiner has parents, which is ordinarily the case, he will probably find that argument to be rather persuasive.

Then again, you could try to persuade your parents not to make you ride a bicycle. You could offer to go to law school instead. Believe it or not, that often works. In the remote instance that it doesn't, however, try suggesting that you may well entertain a recent offer by the best-looking girl in third grade to engage in an illicit affair during recess next week.

Try, also, to remember everything that happens while your parents are teaching you how to ride. Yeah, try to remember how often your dad would swear just because you put your foot down to keep from falling instead of pedaling faster as he wanted. Try to remember all the blood that you lost the one time that you listened to him and didn't put your foot down. Try to remember how guilty you felt when your mother said that if you really cared about them, you would try again. And try to remember how much you hated everyone because everyone learns how to ride a bicycle.

Why should you try to remember? Because it will save your psychiatrist an awful lot of time 20 years later, that's why.

But you should also remember something else: You should remember that there is some justice in this world and that your parents may not realize what they are doing. Yes, any guy who can learn how to ride a bicycle can also learn how to drive a car a few years later.

Just Like Old Times
September 1996

Just Like Old Times

Some of us never really grow up
until we grow old.

I retired from practicing law last year. It wasn't an easy decision, but it was the right one. I wanted to go back home to help my parents, who are both nearly 90 years old.

I'm their only child. And when you're an only child, growing up in the country, you go back home to help your parents when they're older. So that's what I did.

In the process, I learned to like them all over again. It wasn't easy at first. They've changed a lot. But, after a while, I grew to like what they've become. Now that I think about it, I guess they have just become older.

Their house has become older too, but that's different. I never liked that house when I was young. It was out to get me and I knew the reason why: I was an only child and my parents thought that I was special. In fact, they thought that I could do no wrong. The house, however, knew otherwise and was intent on proving it.

So every time I would come in late,

> "You have to get up pretty early in the morning to outsmart a teenage boy."

after everyone was asleep, the insidious little games would start. I would tiptoe around to the back of the house, solely out of consideration for my parents, of course, and try to open the door to the back porch. I say try because I couldn't. No, even when I pulled with both hands, I couldn't. Gosh, I couldn't have opened that door with a crowbar.

Now what's amazing about that is that you could have opened that door with one finger during the daylight hours. My father said that the door expanded after dark. Well, what did fathers know? I knew that the house was deliberately trying to prevent me from sneaking in the back door.

As a result, I would become angry, really angry. I would become so angry that I would pound on the door. That action was designed to cause harm to the door—and it did—a fact my parents would point out right after they stopped yelling at me for coming in so late.

That devious house

had outwitted me again. Obviously I needed a better plan. So I adopted one. The next time I came home late I went straight in the front door.

Teenage boys never come in the front door, not even in the daylight. It's too was a squeaky floorboard. That's right, a board in the floor squeaked just outside the den. You could hardly hear it, but that dog went crazy. You would have thought that someone was trying to steal his doggie treats, which were the only reason he bothered to wake up.

Now let's get something straight: This was not normal. That dog was deaf as a doorpost and lazier than a pig in a wallow. Ordinarily you could not disturb that dog with a shotgun blast. He moved from a yawning position on his rug in the den twice a day: once to go out and once to eat. Otherwise he never moved. I mean, he never even lifted his head. And now he has a barking fit over a squeak in a floorboard that an owl wouldn't have heard even it he were perched right on top of it? Give me a break!

Well, that house was not about to give me a break. It had obviously regrouped and entered into a conspiracy with the dog. Yeah, old Terry, who had been my best childhood friend, had sold me out. He had decided that his quiet spot in the den was more important than the only child in a family that was rapidly beginning to get the wrong impression of him. It made me realize how George Washington must have felt when he learned that Benedict Arnold had tried to sell out West Point to the British during the Revolutionary War.

He felt embarrassed, and so did I. But not nearly as embarrassed as I felt that time in my room when I was 10 and I saw Emilie Ann Hayes walking around in her room next door in her pajamas. That's right, her pajamas! I couldn't believe it. What a terrible thing to do: walk around your room in your pajamas with the window open and without even pulling the blind down. Why, anyone could look in. She was lucky that it was only me. And the only reason that I did was to see if her parents punished her for doing it. I had already learned that it's important to witness justice.

I had also learned that you can witness justice a lot better if you turn your lights out and pull the venetian blinds down so no one can see you watching. That night, though, when I pulled on the cord, the blinds did not come down slowly as they had always done before: They fell with a thud right on top of my nose. I screamed and so did Emilie Ann— but not nearly as loud as my parents did when they rushed into the room and realized what had happened.

No matter how hard I tried to explain for the next month, during which I was not allowed to leave that malicious house, my parents just did not understand. Obviously they had a different concept of justice than I did—and it did not include Emilie Ann Hayes.

I guess the only thing that really changes when you grow old is your way of looking at everything. When you're older you really can't see what things are like very well anymore. Your heart gets in the way.

The Wind Beneath My Wings
November 1996

The Wind Beneath My Wings

Trying to get to heaven on the
end of a kite string.

I hate doing homework. I've always hated doing homework. The only reason that I did it was because my mother told me in elementary school that I would never get anywhere without doing it. So I did.

But I could never finish. The assignments were always too long. How could they expect you to finish all that work in just 10 minutes? It was unrealistic. And like every other 10-year-old boy in central Pennsylvania, I was realistic. So I would always spend the last five minutes thinking about the windy afternoons I would fly kites from the lookout at Price Park. It was perched out on a cliff overlooking the West Branch of the Susquehanna River, which was immediately below, and my hometown, which was situated along the southern shore a few miles downstream.

I would always send those kites up into the wind blowing downriver toward the town. They would soar, and so would I, toward the clouds and the town, where only hours earlier I had seemed nothing more than yet another 10-year-old boy. But not now, though. Now I was something special. And now I was especially interested in having Barbara Dilling see that fact.

She was the best-looking girl in fifth grade at old Roosevelt Elementary School. At least all the boys thought so. But they, the other boys, were all bigger than I was, and Barbara was, too. So I couldn't even hope—until I flew my kite. Then it was different: I grew a few feet.

Big? She wanted big? Well, I'd give her big! Forget six feet tall—I'd give her 6,000 feet tall!

The only trouble was that I was up so high that she couldn't even see me. But then, no one could over at the girls' locker room at the high school, either, so I always decided to drift over there next.

That locker room's skylight was the principal subject of conversation of all my friends' older brothers. Yet I never could understand what their interest was. That locker room was for girls and any 10-year-old boy in my town could tell you that there was nothing very interesting about girls—with the possible exception of Barbara Dilling. No, there had to be something else down there-something sinister like a secret society or a cult.

Actually, that locker room may have been the place where all the girls regularly met to decide how they would make boys' lives miserable. You know, by always doing their homework on time, by knowing the answers to the questions in class all the time, by never talking in Sunday School, by never getting dirty even when they played outside, and, in very rare cases, by sort of looking kind of cute—like Barbara Dilling.

Gee, for all I knew, Barbara Dilling may have been their chieftain. Sure, for some time she had been sort of cozying up to Butch Winner, Wally Smith, Jan Bennett, and Buddy Beers, who were either the biggest, toughest, or best-looking guys in the class. Maybe she was trying to capture one of them to take back to her girlfriends in the locker room to use as a human sacrifice. Gosh, maybe it was not so bad to be the littlest guy in fifth grade after all.

Well, I planned to expose the whole sordid mess once I got my kite up and over that skylight. That way I might be able to at least save Wally and Butch, who were two of my best friends.

Oh, I knew there would be repercussions. You could tell from watching the older kids walk home from high school that girls only went steady with boys that liked them. And after I exposed this mess, every girl in the world would realize that I didn't particularly like any one of them—with the possible exception of Barbara Dilling, which I couldn't really explain. And once they learned that, they probably wouldn't want to marry me.

Well, I didn't care. I would rather have married Butch or Wally anyway. Everybody always said that the person you marry should be your best friend.

Everybody also said that 10-year-old boys should do everything they can to get to heaven. Well, all I did was let out enough string. Yeah, when you let out enough string, you can soar all the way up to heaven. And when you do, you can see that there are only 10-year-old boys up there—no girls. Not even Barbara Dilling. Well, maybe Barbara Dilling—and my mother, too. But no others. Even better, all the little 10-year-old boys grew taller so that they were just as tall as every other 10-year-old boy, and taller than Barbara Dilling. And in heaven, Barbara Dilling decided to go steady with the worst-looking one of them.

Yeah, you learn a lot of things flying kites. But the most important thing you learn is that, no matter what everybody says, you don't have to do your homework to get somewhere.

www.ingramcontent.com/pod-product-compliance
Lightning Source LLC
Chambersburg PA
CBHW020242010526
44107CB00039B/1463/J